PowerShell

The ultimate beginners guide to learn PowerShell step-by-step

Mark Reed

Table of Contents

Introduction

Computer system administration can be difficult, especially when you deal with large or complex computing systems. Even in the case where systems are smaller and less complex, routine maintenance can also represent another challenge. PowerShell is a system administration and configuration technology that is designed specifically to address these challenges.

Learning a new technology within the fast and vast field of computing system administration can be daunting and very difficult, especially when involved technologies are both fast-changing and difficult to grasp. In these situations, it is useful to have a comprehensive guide that can help you learn the most important components of the technology in question quickly. In addition, the guide should summarize the learning items into a compact set that can help you translate the technology into everyday use.

This is precisely what this book is for PowerShell 7.0 does for beginners. This book will provide you, as the reader, with a comprehensive foundation to a new and exciting technology in the form of PowerShell 7.0. This book has the crisp rigor of computer programming presented in a compact manner while maintaining the full comprehensive scope. The ideas presented here capture the best system administration and configuration technologies from the fast-changing landscape of the Microsoft .NET platform. These ideas are presented to you in a manner that is easy to learn so that you can quickly put them into practical use.

After reading this book, you can begin to use the most important technologies in PowerShell 7.0 right away. This will not only improve how you manage computing systems in the present computing landscape, but also how you will adapt to future developments.

PowerShell is a part of some of the most important Microsoft certifications ("Online IT Training Videos, IT Certification Training | CBT Nuggets", 2019), including Microsoft Certified Solutions Associate: Windows Server 2016, Microsoft Certified Solutions Expert: Productivity, Microsoft Certified: Azure Administrator and MCSE: Mobility.

There are nine categories of scripting languages and roughly 192 languages in total ("Scripting Languages", 2018), with each language evolving in line with the fast-paced developments in the field of computer software. PowerShell became open-source in 2016, thus laying the foundation for the language to evolve at an extremely fast pace. This book will equip you with the skills to not only quickly go from a beginner to an intermediate in one of these languages but also to put the language to practical use very quickly.

PowerShell 7.0 utilizes the latest developments in Microsoft .NET platform stack architecture in the form of the Standard 2.0 library and the .NET Core 3.1 stack ("Announcing The Powershell 7.0 Release Candidate | Powershell", 2019). This book will help you learn how to put to practical use the most important components of these developments within PowerShell 7.0 instantly. Not only will you begin creating custom administration and configuration tools for your computing environments, but you will be able to do so for future PowerShell versions as well.

PowerShell 7.0 can be utilized in various operating system environments (Windows, Linux, and macOS environments), both in local environments and in the cloud. This book will effortlessly equip you with the compact set of requisite knowledge to utilize PowerShell 7.0 in each of these environments in no time.

I can promise that with this book, you will be automating repetitive tasks, running custom encryption protocols, and overseeing large-scale management over complex computing systems effortlessly in little to no time at all. In addition, you will be able to use many of the solutions to real-world problems outlined in this book in your day-to-day tasks (Arntzen, 2019).

It is imperative to remember, however, that any computing system, even a simple example such as your laptop, will continue to grow more complex and difficult to manage with time. The solution to most of your problems may be outlined in the next pages.

Chapter One:
PowerShell Components

In this chapter we will explore the components of PowerShell 7.0. The components of PowerShell are the user interface (UI) with which users interact with PowerShell as well as related software that houses PowerShell components used to enhance the user interface. The related software comprises Visual Studio Code (VS Code) and the PowerShell Gallery. VS Code is a script editor that houses PowerShell integrated scripting environment features. The PowerShell Gallery is a PowerShell content central repository which can be accessed from PowerShell. In this chapter we will also go through the steps of downloading and installing the first two components (namely, PowerShell and VS Code). The installation instructions assume that you have an internet connection.

PowerShell 7.0 is a GitHub project that was made open source in 2016, and this chapter will look at how to source material available on GitHub when starting PowerShell 7.0. The main PowerShell 7.0 installation method described for the Windows and Linux operating systems uses the .NET Core SDK (Software Development Kit). In the case of macOS, the main method is by direct download, but the .NET Core SDK method will also be described. In the case of

ARM, (Acorn RISC Machine) devices, a Windows method and a Linux method will be outlined.

Installing PowerShell 7.0 on Windows

The simplest method to install PowerShell 7.0 on Windows is to use the .NET Core SDK ("Installing Powershell Core On Windows - Powershell", 2019).

The first step is to have .NET Core SDK installed. This is done by downloading an installer for your Computer Processing Unit (CPU), namely, (x64 or x86) from https://dotnet.microsoft.com/download/dotnet-core/3.1 ("Install .NET Core SDK On Windows, Linux, And macOS - .NET Core", 2019).

The second step is to run the installer and follow the Wizard prompts. The third step is to check that everything installed properly by opening a command prompt and running this command (".NET Tutorial | Hello World In 10 Minutes", 2019):

>dotnet

If "dotnet" results in a dotnet help file printout, then the installation ran successfully. If the command results in an error command stating that dotnet is not recognized as a command, then try re-opening the command prompt.

The fourth step is to run this command to install PowerShell as a .NET Global tool ("Installing Powershell Core On Windows - Powershell", 2019):

>dotnet tool install --global PowerShell

The remainder of the methods can be found at:

https://docs.microsoft.com/en-us/powershell/scripting/install/installing-powershell-core-on-windows?view=powershell-7

Installing PowerShell 7.0 on Linux

PowerShell 7.0 support is available for Ubuntu (16.04, 18.04, 18.10 and 19.04), Debian (8.9.10), CentOS 7, Fedora (27,28), Red Hat Enterprise Linux (RHEL) 7, openSUSE (42.3, LEAP 15) and Arch Linux ("Installing Powershell Core On Linux - Powershell", 2019). The simplest method to install PowerShell 7.0 on Linux is to use the .NET Core SDK ("Installing Powershell Core On Linux - Powershell", 2019).

The first step is to install the .NET Core SDK. This is done by downloading a binary for your Linux distribution from https://dotnet.microsoft.com/download/dotnet-core/3.1. Then issue the following commands on the terminal ("Installing Powershell Core On Linux - Powershell", 2019):

$mkdir -p $HOME/dotnet && tar zxf dotnet-sdk-3.1.100-linux-x64.tar.gz -C $HOME/dotnet

$export DOTNET_ROOT=$HOME/dotnet

$export PATH=$PATH:$HOME/dotnet

The preceding exports in the last commands are temporary. In other words, the .NET Core Command Line Interface (CLI) features are available only for that session. However, the commands can be made permanent by first editing the shell profile. In different Linux shells, the following profiles can be edited ("Installing Powershell Core On Linux - Powershell", 2019):

- Bash Shell: the ~/.bash_profile and ~/.bashrc

- Korn Shell: ~/.kshrc or .profile

- Z Shell: the ~/.zshrc or .zprofile

Then complete the update by updating the shell source file by adding $HOME/dotnet at the end of the PATH statement. If there is no PATH statement in the file, then add the following new line:

export PATH=$PATH:$HOME/dotnet

and

DOTNET_ROOT=$HOME/dotnet

at the end of the file.

The third step is to check that everything installed properly by opening a command prompt and running this command (".NET Tutorial | Hello World In 10 Minutes", 2019):

$dotnet

If the script results in a dotnet help file printout, then the installation ran successfully. If the command results in an error command stating that dotnet is not recognized as a command, then try re-opening the command prompt. The next step is to run this command to install PowerShell as a .NET Global tool ("Installing Powershell Core On Linux - Powershell", 2019):

$ dotnet tool install --global PowerShell

The preceding steps are used across all Linux distributions. The following link describes the installation steps for each distribution and version supported by PowerShell 7.0. The Linux distribution-specific methods can be found at https://docs.microsoft.com/en-us/powershell/scripting/install/installing-powershell-core-on-linux?view=powershell-7#ubuntu-1810

Installing PowerShell 7.0 on macOS

On macOS, the simplest method is to install PowerShell 7.0.0 directly from the release page by downloading the macOS package from ("Installing Powershell Core On Macos - Powershell", 2019) https://github.com/PowerShell/PowerShell/releases/latest.

Once PowerShell is installed, issue the following command ("Installing Powershell Core On Macos - Powershell", 2019):

$pwsh

The next best method is to install PowerShell using the .NET Core SDK ("Installing Powershell Core On macOS - Powershell", 2019). The first step is to download the installer from ("Install .NET Core SDK On Windows, Linux, And Macos - .NET Core", 2019) https://dotnet.microsoft.com/download/dotnet-core/3.1.

Then use the macOS standalone installer command prompts to install the .NET Core 3.1 SDK. The third step is to check that everything installed properly by opening a command prompt and running the following command (".NET Tutorial | Hello World In 10 Minutes", 2019):

$dotnet

If it results in a dotnet help file printout, then the installation ran successfully. If the command results in an error command stating that dotnet is not recognized as a command, try re-opening the command prompt.

The fourth step is to install PowerShell as a .NET Global tool ("Installing Powershell Core On Macos - Powershell", 2019) with the following command:

$dotnet tool install --global PowerShell

The remainder of the methods for installing PowerShell on macOS can be found at https://docs.microsoft.com/en-us/powershell/scripting/install/installing-powershell-core-on-macos?view=powershell-7

Installing PowerShell 7.0.0 on ARM

PowerShell 7.0 can be used on a limited set of ARM devices, which include Windows 10 ARM32/ARM64 as well as Raspbian. PowerShell 7.0 for ARM is an unsupported experimental release. In this section we will consider the installation instructions for Raspbian and Windows 10 Internet of Things (IoT).

Deployment on Windows IoT

The installation instructions for deploying on Windows IoT are as follows ("Installing Powershell Core On Windows - Powershell", 2019):

Windows IoT has Windows PowerShell pre-installed, which can be used in the installation of PowerShell 7.0.0-rc.1.

1. Creation of PSSession to device

   $s = New-PSSession -ComputerName <deviceIp> -Credential Administrator

2. Copy ZIP package to device

   # change the destination to however you had partitioned it with sufficient

   # space for the zip and the unzipped contents

   # the path should be local to the device

   Copy-Item .\PowerShell-<version>-win-<os-arch>.zip -Destination u:\users\administrator\Downloads -ToSession $s

3. Connect to device and extract the archive

   Enter-PSSession $s

   Set-Location u:\users\administrator\downloads

   Expand-Archive .\PowerShell-<version>-win-<os-arch>.zip

4. Remoting setup to PowerShell 7.0.0-rc.1

   Set-Location .\PowerShell-<version>-win-<os-arch>

   # Be sure to use the -PowerShellHome parameter otherwise it'll try to create a new

   # endpoint with Windows PowerShell 5.1

.\Install-PowerShellRemoting.ps1   -
PowerShellHome .

You'll get an error message and will be disconnected from the device because it has to restart WinRM

5.   Connect to PowerShell Core 7.0 device endpoint

Be sure to use the -Configuration parameter. If you omit it, you will connect to Windows PowerShell 5.1

Enter-PSSession -ComputerName <deviceIp> -Credential   Administrator   -Configuration powershell.<version>

Installing on Raspbian

The installation on Raspbian is done by running the following sequence of commands ("Installing Powershell Core On Linux - Powershell", 2019):

#####################################

Prerequisites

Update package lists

sudo apt-get update

Install libunwind8 and libssl1.0

Regex is used to ensure that we do not install libssl1.0-dev, as it is a variant that is not required

16

```
sudo apt-get install '^libssl1.0.[0-9]$' libunwind8 -y

#######################################
# Download and extract PowerShell

# Grab the latest tar.gz
wget https://github.com/PowerShell/PowerShell/releases/download/v7.0.0/powershell-7.0.0-linux-arm32.tar.gz

# Make folder to put powershell
mkdir ~/powershell

# Unpack the tar.gz file
tar -xvf ./powershell-7.0.0-linux-arm32.tar.gz -C ~/powershell

# Start PowerShell
~/powershell/pwsh
```

The remainder of the Raspbian installation instructions can be found at https://docs.microsoft.com/en-us/powershell/scripting/install/installing-powershell-core-on-linux?view=powershell-7#raspbian

PowerShell Console

In this section we will briefly consider the PowerShell Console. The PowerShell Console is a very important PowerShell component because most of the scripting will be done using the console. Later, when discussing Visual Studio Code, we will explore how the console can be linked to the Visual Studio Code environment.

The command line options used to start PowerShell can also customize the session and control the input. These features will be explored in later sections and chapters as they arise. In this exploratory tour, we can consider the basic PowerShell command line interface which will appear as follows in Windows under the C:\ path:

PS C:\>

and analogously, according to command line system file representation, for Linux and macOS under /home/user/ path:

PS /home/user/>

The basic convention in this book will be to represent the PowerShell 7.0 command line prompt as follows:

>

However, output obtained for PowerShell running in one operating system is translatable to an analogous output obtained via another operating system.

A simple administrative command to run on the console is to invoke the Get-Process cmdlet. The cmdlet displays management information on local or remote computer processes or. The PowerShell Console command to invoke the cmdlet is:

>Get-Process

The output obtained is as follows (where only the first few lines are shown):

PS C:\> Get-Process

Handles	NPM(K)	PM(K)	WS(K)	CPU(s)	Id	SI	ProcessName
-------	------	-----	-----	------	--	--	-----------
524	29	21876	16508	1.64	52736	0	AbtSvcHost_
370	18	3880	2356	3.23	3532	0	armsvc
204	12	9920	13424	0.14	47940	0	audiodg
326	31	14596	34876	0.33	13960	219	backgroundTaskHost
284	20	11776	25393	0.47	47300	216	backgroundTaskHost
133	9	2380	988	0.11	15092	0	CNTAoSMgr

The cmdlet invoked without parameter entries obtains management information on local computer processes. As you will see in the next chapter, the default mode invocation of the Get-Process cmdlet yields, for each process, an object with process management information. The Get-Process cmdlet also provides support for methods for starting and stopping the process.

This is the default method of interacting with Powershell via the console. PowerShell has more than 1900 cmdlets ("Powershell", 2020) and the basic method to invoke their functionalities, in a computing system environment using PowerShell, is through the console.

Visual Studio Code

In this section of PowerShell components, we will explore the Visual Studio Code installation and setup processes on Windows, Linux, and macOS. This section will also discuss how to locate the PowerShell Extension Code via examples. The setup process will include installing extensions for C#, .NET Core, and PowerShell.

The extension installations will also provide brief illustrations on how to use the extensions. In this light, the PowerShell extension installation will include a pointer on how to access the VS Code PowerShell examples. Similarly, for the remaining extensions, the section will end with a brief VS Code demonstration with C# and .NET Core.

The instructions for installing VS Code and VS Code extensions on your operating system (Windows, Linux and macOS) are available from:

https://code.visualstudio.com/docs/setup/setup-overview

Figure 1 below shows an empty template of the VS Code development environment.

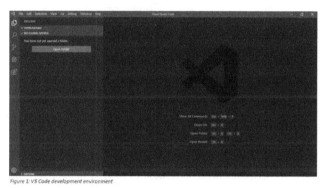

Figure 1: VS Code development environment

Installing the PowerShell Extension

When looking to use VS Code with PowerShell, the first step after installing VS Code is to install the PowerShell extension. The PowerShell extension for VS Code provides language support for PowerShell versions 3.0 and upward ("PowerShell Editing With Visual Studio Code, 2019). The capabilities added by the extension include linting analysis, definition tracking, and completions.

In order to install the extension, browse and install the extension from VS Code using the Extensions menu. On the left hand side of the VS Code window, find the Activity Bar and click on the Extensions icon. The Extensions icon appears as a four block icon consisting of three connected blocks and a detached fourth block located on the VS Code left hand icon menu bar. Alternatively, use the View: Extensions command (Ctrl+Shift+X or Cmd+Shift+X), which will show a list of the most popular VS Code extensions on the VS Code Marketplace ("Managing Extensions In Visual Studio Code", 2019).

code --install-extension myextension.vsix

The third method is to install the PowerShell extension externally from VS Code using a command line tool (PowerShell, Cmd.exe, or bash) with the following command ("Powershell Editing With Visual Studio Code", 2019):

code --install-extension ms-vscode.powershell

In VS Code Insiders edition, the command changes to:

code-insiders --install-extension ms-vscode.powershell

Example PowerShell Scripts

Example PowerShell extension scripts can be found using the path ("Powershell Editing With Visual Studio Code", 2019):

C:\Users\<yourusername>\.vscode\extensions\ms-vscode.PowerShell-<version>\examples

Here, <version> stands for the extension version.

Open the example scripts in VS Code by running the following command in either PowerShell or the command prompt ("Powershell Editing With Visual Studio Code", 2019):

code   (Get-ChildItem $Home\.vscode\extensions\ms-vscode.PowerShell-*\examples)[-1]

If using VS Code Insiders, run:

$Home\.vscode-insiders\extensions\ms-vscode.PowerShell-*\examples)[-1]

Another option is to open the examples using the Command Palette loaded by pressing (Ctrl+Shift+P or Cmd+Shift+P) and selecting "PowerShell: Open Examples Folder" from the available commands.

Installing the C# extension and .NET Core extension pack

The C# extension and the .NET Core extension pack can also be installed analogously to the

PowerShell extension. The .NET Core extension pack includes the C# extension and other extensions related to .NET Core.

Bonus Exercise: Create a .NET Core Application with .NET Core SDK , Visual Studio Code with C# extension, and Visual Studio .NET Core extension pack

If you did not install PowerShell using the .NET SDK option in the installation, follow the installation instructions for the .NET Core SDK outlined in that section and then continue with this exercise. If you did not install either the VS Code C# extension or the .NET Core extension pack, then install at least one of these and then continue with this exercise.

.NET Core is a modular platform for developing server apps that can be deployed across operating systems (Linux, macOS, and Windows) (".NET Core And Visual Studio Code", 2019). The C# VS Code extension adds full C# IntelliSense debugging and support to VS Code script editing.

In the following exercise we will use the VS Code editor, .NET Core SDK, and the command prompt (Cmd.exe). In addition, we will use either the VS Code C# extension or the VS Code .NET Core extension.

These are the steps for building a dotnet "Hello World" application (".NET Core And Visual Studio Code", 2019):

Step 1: C# project initialization.

Start a command shell, create a directory for your Hello World application, and navigate to the directory by typing the following:

> cd C:\

> mkdir Apps

> cd Apps

> dotnet new console

The steps and output on the command prompt will be as shown in Figure 2 below.

Figure 2: .NET Core application command prompt output

25

Step 2: Open VS Code and navigate to the project folder.

The VS Code console will be as shown in Figure 3 below.

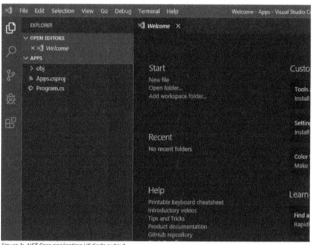

Figure 3: .NET Core application VS Code output

Step 3: Running the application.

The application can be run with the following command prompt command:

> dotnet run

This will generate the output shown in Figure 4 below.

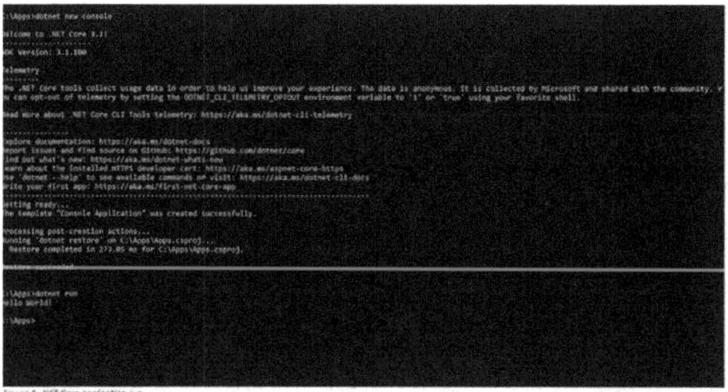

Figure 4: .NET Core application run

PowerShell Gallery

The PowerShell Gallery is a package repository containing modules, scripts, and Desired State Configuration (DSC) resources ("Get Started With The Powershell Gallery - Powershell", 2019). These are available for download and leverage. The PowerShellGet module has cmdlets that can be used to explore and install these packages. Cmdlets will be covered in Chapter Two: Commands. A PowerShell Gallery item download does not require signing into the gallery. The PowerShell Gallery will be covered in Chapter Eight: Remoting.

The PowerShell Gallery Search control can be used to search for packages on the homepage (https://www.powershellgallery.com/) or to search through scripts and modules in the packages webpage (https://www.powershellgallery.com/packages).

As we will consider in Chapter Eight, PowerShell Gallery packages can be obtained using the Find-

Module, Find-Script and Find-DscResource cmdlets, depending on the package type, with parameter - Repository PSGallery. Result filtering can use the following parameter list: AllVersions, Command, DscResource, Filter, Includes, MinimumVersion, Name, Tag, and RequiredVersion.

The Find-Dscresource cmdlet can be used for discovering DSC resources. The cmdlet returns information on Gallery DSC resources. DSC resources are packaged in a module, and thus after the resource is found, it can be installed using the Install-Module cmdlet.

Exercises

1.1. What are the main methods to run the PowerShell Console?

1.2. What are the three VS Code extensions considered in the Chapter?

1.3. Is it possible to run the PowerShell Console from within VS Code? If so, how?

1.4. What PowerShell module can be used to install packages from the PowerShell Gallery?

1.5. Why is the PowerShell Gallery useful when using PowerShell 7.0?

1.6. How do you install the PowerShell extension from within VS Code using a .vsix file?

Chapter Summary

The key points of the chapter were:

- PowerShell 7.0 has operating system and environment specific installation procedures.

- The .NET Core SDK based installation process is the simplest across all supported platforms.

- The main components of PowerShell 7.0 are the PowerShell Console, Visual Studio Code, and the PowerShell Gallery.

- The Console and Visual Studio Code components can be linked using the Visual Studio Code PowerShell extension.

- The main components of PowerShell constitute the GUI with which users interact with PowerShell.

- The PowerShellGallery component houses a lot of PowerShell features that can be used to enhance the basic installation when the setting requires so.

In the next chapter you will learn about PowerShell commands and how they are issued in PowerShell when using various components in your computing environment activities.

Chapter Two:
Commands

A command is a task-specific instruction to a computer program ("Command (Computing)", 2019). A cmdlet is a minimal version of a command utilized within PowerShell ("Cmdlet Overview - Powershell", 2019). In PowerShell, cmdlets can be invoked at PowerShell runtime as part of automation scripts issued on the PowerShell console or PowerShell Application Programming Interface (API) programs.

PowerShell modules, which will be covered in Chapter Six, provide a way to package cmdlets into groups based on function ("Powershell Scripting - Powershell", 2019). Table 1 below describes these modules (or groups) and their functions.

The three modules or cmdlet groups that immediately stand out are the Microsoft.PowerShell.Core, Microsoft.PowerShell. Utility, and Microsoft.PowerShell.Host modules. The first two module groups deal with the core functions and basic features of PowerShell, respectively. The third module deals with logging records. The next two module groups to consider are Microsoft.PowerShell.Security and Microsoft. PowerShell.Management. The activities associated with these two module groups can be paired with the description of the Microsoft.PowerShell.Diagnostics.

The activities associated with module groups Microsoft.PowerShell.Diagnostics, PSDesiredStateConfiguration, and PSDiagnostics can be easily grouped together. The activities of Microsoft.WSMan.management and CIMcmdlets can also be grouped together.

The activities of PSDesiredStateConfiguration, ThreadJob, PowerShellGet, PackageManagement, and Microsoft.PowerShell.Archive could be grouped together in some settings. The PSReadLine module contains cmdlets that help with command-line editing analogous to script editor support in scripting.

Cmdlet module group	Group Function
CimCmdlets	Contains cmdlets that interact with Common Information Model (CIM) Servers like the Windows Management Instrumentation (WMI) service.
Microsoft.PowerShell.Archive	The Microsoft.PowerShell.Archive module contains cmdlets that let you create and extract archive or ZIP files.
Microsoft.PowerShell.Diagnostics	The PowerShell Microsoft.PowerShell.Diagnostics module contains cmdlets that manage data from event logs
Microsoft.PowerShell.Core	The Microsoft.PowerShell.Core module contains cmdlets and providers that manage the basic features of PowerShell.
Microsoft.PowerShell.Host	The Microsoft.PowerShell.Host module contains cmdlets that manage data from host programs.
Microsoft.PowerShell.Management	The Microsoft.PowerShell.Host module contains cmdlets that manage data from host programs.
Microsoft.PowerShell.Security	The Microsoft.PowerShell.Security module contains cmdlets and providers that manage the basic security features.
Microsoft.PowerShell.Utility	The Microsoft.PowerShell.Utility module contains cmdlets that manage the basic features of PowerShell.
Microsoft.WSMan.Management	Microsoft.WSMan.Management module contains cmdlets and providers that manage the WS-Management (Web Services-management) protocol in PowerShell.
PackageManagement	The PackageManagement module contains cmdlets that are used for package management.
PowerShellGet	PowerShellGet is a module with cmdlets for discovering, installing, updating and publishing PowerShell artifacts like Modules, DSC (Desired State Configuration) Resources, Role Capabilities, and Scripts.
PSDesiredStateConfiguration	The PSDesiredStateConfiguration (PowerShell Desired State Configuration) module contains cmdlets that designed to work with DSC Resources.
PSDiagnostics	The PSDiagnostics (PowerShell Diagnostics) module contains a set of cmdlets that enables the use of Event Tracing for Windows (ETW) tracing in PowerShell.
PSReadLine	The PowerShell Read Line (PSReadLine) module contains cmdlets that let you customize the command-line editing environment in PowerShell.
ThreadJob	The ThreadJob module extends the existing PowerShell BackgroundJob to include a new thread based ThreadJob job. This is a lighter weight solution for running concurrent PowerShell scripts that works within the existing PowerShell job infrastructure.

Table 1: Cmdlet Module descriptions

31

It is worth highlighting , however, that archiving is also closely related to the activity associated with Microsoft.PowerShell.Management, depending on whether the user is creating or opening the archives.

In order to better contextualize the use of cmdlets, it is imperative to approach cmdlets from the perspective of a computing systems administrator. A system administrator controls the maintenance, reliable functioning, and configuration of computing systems within multi-user computing system environments such as computer clusters ("System Administrator", 2019). A system administrator safeguards the security, resources, uptime, and performance of the computing systems he or she oversees while meeting user needs according to a prescribed budget.

System administrators typically perform the following tasks:

- User account management

- Operating system management

- System log analysis

- Systems analysis and potential issue identification

- Safeguarding network infrastructure uptime

- New software and hardware installation

- Safeguarding security

- File system management

- Computer system physical environment management and planning

- Safeguarding computer environment (production, test, and development) parity

- Documenting system configuration

- Problem troubleshooting

- User training

- Setting system performance

- Technical support and user assistance

In a PowerShell introduction it is imperative to keep in mind the activities of a system administrator and the PowerShell tools available in the form of the cmdlets arranged into modules available to perform the tasks of a system administrator.

The next step is to look at the technical components of cmdlets. Please note that this part of a PowerShell introduction may seem difficult at first. Please make sure to work through this section many times. Once you fully understand this section, most other aspects of PowerShell will be relatively easy to understand.

The first step in understanding cmdlets is to understand the cmdlet structure.

In the following section, please keep in mind the concept of a C# class object and also refer to the example at the end of the section to identify the component described in the structure. The purpose of this section is to outline the structure rather than emphasize on its specifics. It is not necessary to know all the .NET classes, protocols, and APIs, but it is important to have an understanding of the objects that the cmdlet interacts with when performing its function.

Cmdlet Structure

In simple terms, cmdlets are objects that perform an action or method and yield a .NET Framework object to a following command in a pipeline. Pipelines will be covered in detail in the next chapter. A written cmdlet class is a derived cmdlet class implementation of one of two base classes (Microsoft Doc 2019). These two base classes, in turn, are specialized cmdlet classes.

The derived class is required to:

- Include a declaration of an attribute giving it the identity of a cmdlet.

- Have public property definitions that can be recognized with attributes used to identify the defined properties to be cmdlet parameters.

- Override at least one method for processing input in record-processing.

34

After implementing the derived class, the assembly containing the class must be directly loaded into the PowerShell environment either by using the Import-Module cmdlet or by creating a host application to load the assembly through the System.Management.Automation.Runspaces.Initialses sionstate API. These two approaches provide console and program access to cmdlet functionality in PowerShell.

This functional description of the cmdlet class allows us to characterize the cmdlet structure through a set of cmdlet terms.

Cmdlet Terms

These terms can be used to characterize the structure of a cmdlet ("Cmdlet Overview - Powershell", 2019):

- Cmdlet Attribute

This is a required .NET attribute used in the declaration of a derived cmdlet class. A cmdlet must have this feature to be a PowerShell cmdlet. In addition to the cmdlet attribute, PowerShell also allows the cmdlet to have other optional attributes.

- Cmdlet Parameter

This is a cmdlet public property defining the parameters available to users or applications that will run the cmdlet. The parameters may be required, positional, named, or switch, and will be shown in the core command syntax section.

- Dynamic Parameter

This is a cmdlet parameter available only at runtime when certain requirements are met.

- Parameter Set

This is a parameter collection supplied to a single command to complete an explicit action. As will be seen in the command syntax section below, a cmdlet may have more than one parameter set, but each parameter set has a minimum of one unique parameter. A well-designed cmdlet has unique parameters that are also required parameters.

- Methods for Processing Input

This is a cmdlet input-record processing method. Available methods include System.Management.Automation.Cmdlet.BeginProcessing, System.Management.Automation.Cmdlet.EndProcessing, System.Management.Automation.Cmdlet.ProcessRecord, and System.Management.Automation.Cmdlet.StopProcessing. The cmdlet is required to override at least one of the first three during implementation. Usually it overrides System.Management.Automation.Cmdlet.ProcessRec ord, since this method is required by the cmdlet for every processed record. The first method is required once to execute record pre-processing. The second is, analogously, required once for record post-processing.

- Transaction

Transactions are commands that are arranged into a logical unit and handled as one task. The properties of the command unit are firstly that the whole task is treated as failed if one command in the unit fails. Secondly, it is at the user's discretion to reject or accept the individual commands within a transaction. The cmdlets are required to declare transaction support as part of the cmdlet attribute declaration.

- ShouldProcess Feature

PowerShell cmdlets can be designed to request user feedback before making system changes. The design has two components. The first component requires that the cmdlet make a ShouldProcess feature declaration during cmdlet attribute declaration. The second component requires that the cmdlet call the System.Management.Automation.Cmdlet.ShouldCoun tine and System.Management.Automation.Cmdlet.ShouldProc ess methods inside an input processing method.

How Cmdlets Vary from Commands

Cmdlets vary from commands in other command-line interfaces in that cmdlets:

- Are .NET Framework class instances rather than stand-alone executables.

- Are constructed from code of varying lengths.

- Do not perform their own parsing, output formatting, or error presentation. In PowerShell, these actions are conducted by the runtime.

- Process pipeline input objects rather than text streams, and they usually deliver pipeline output objects.

- Do single object processing in each instance, thus making them record-oriented.

Cmdlet Base Classes

PowerShell allows cmdlets to derive from these base classes:

- The System.Management.Automation.Cmdlet base class: Cmdlets deriving from this base class use the minimal collection of PowerShell runtime dependencies. The main benefits of this are twofold. First, it makes for smaller cmdlet objects impacted less by PowerShell runtime changes. The second is that cmdlet object instances can be created and invoked directly without requiring the object's PowerShell runtime invocation.

- The System.Management.Automation.PSCmdlet: This is used for more complex cmdlets with greater access to the PowerShell runtime. The greater access in turn allows for the calling of scripts, accessing of providers, and accessing of the present session state. The state of the current session is accessed by obtaining and setting session preferences and variables. In this case, the cmdlet object is larger and more impacted by changes to the PowerShell runtime.

When extended PowerShell runtime access is not required, then the cmdlet should derive from the System.Management.Automation.Cmdlet class. The benefit of utilizing the PowerShell runtime is its increased cmdlet execution logging facilities. Hence, deriving from this base class allows you to use this facility to run logging-dependent auditing models. In addition, deriving from the base class can be used to stop a cmdlet from executing inside another cmdlet.

Methods For Processing Input

The virtual record processing methods offered by the System.Management.Automation.Cmdlet class are:

- System.Management.Automation.Cmdlet.BeginProcessing: This method provides a one-time pre-processing function. It is optional.

- System.Management.Automation.Cmdlet.End Processing: This method provides a one-time post-processing function. It is optional.

- System.Management.Automation.Cmdlet.Proc essRecord: This method provides a record-by-record processing function. Its calls are mainly input-dependent. The frequency of its calls may be zero or arbitrary.

-

  System.Management.Automation.Cmdlet.Stop Processing: This method provides a stop-processing function. For example, this method would be called when the user presses CTRL+C to stop cmdlet processing.

Derived cmdlets have to override at least one of the first three methods during implementation.

Cmdlet Attributes

These are .NET attributes for managing cmdlets. They are used by cmdlets to specify and access required common functionalities offered by PowerShell.

Cmdlet Names

PowerShell cmdlets are named using verb-noun pairs. The noun specifies the computer resource the cmdlet will act on and the verb specifies the action the cmdlet will take. Cmdlet names are defined as part of the .NET class cmdlet declaration.

Cmdlet Structure Example

It is imperative at this stage to give specific form to this information with an example. Our example will explore the structure of a cmdlet from a programming perspective. The cmdlet is called a Send-Greeting cmdlet obtained from "How To Write A Simple Cmdlet - Powershell" (2019). The Send-Greeting cmdlet has a –Name input parameter that takes the user's name and outputs the greeting on the console. The cmdlet performs a very simple task but satisfies all the requirements of a cmdlet that we have previously explored.

In line with the structural requirements outlined above, let us consider the steps involved in writing a cmdlet, which are as follows:

Step One: Use the Cmdlet attribute to declare the derived class as a cmdlet. The Cmdlet attribute gives the cmdlet name verb-noun combination.

Step Two: Provide the name of the class.

Step Three: Specify that the cmdlet derives from one of the following cmdlet base classes: System.Management.Automation.PSCmdlet or System.Management.Automation.Cmdlet

Step Four: Use the Parameter attribute to specify the cmdlet parameter (-Name)

Step Five: Override one of the required methods for input processing. In this example, we choose to override System.Management.Automation.Cmdlet.ProcessRecord.

Step Six: Format the output object. Use the System.Management.Automation.Cmdlet.WriteObject to specify the greeting display format:

Hello <UserName>!

These steps are performed by using the C# code shown in Figure 5 below ("How To Write A Simple Cmdlet - Powershell", 2019). The structural description coupled with the cmdlet creation method provides the basis for understanding PowerShell cmdlets and how they behave in the PowerShell components.

Send_Greeting.cs

```
using System.Management.Automation;  // PowerShell assembly.

namespace SendGreeting

{

// Declare the class as a cmdlet and specify the

// appropriate verb and noun for the cmdlet name.

[Cmdlet(VerbsCommunications.Send, "Greeting")]

public class SendGreetingCommand : Cmdlet

{

// Declare the parameters for the cmdlet.

[Parameter(Mandatory=true)]

public string Name

{

  get { return name; }

  set { name = value; }

}

private string name;

// Override the ProcessRecord method to process

// the supplied user name and write out a

// greeting to the user by calling the WriteObject

// method.

protected override void ProcessRecord()

{

  WriteObject("Hello " + name + "!");

}

}

}
```

Figure 5: Greetings cmdlet program

The syntax for obtaining more information about a cmdlet is:

>Get-Help <cmdlet-name>

This brings us to the concept of PowerShell syntax diagrams.

Syntax Diagrams

Commands in PowerShell are constructed with the help of syntax diagram displays ("About_Command_Syntax - Powershell", 2020). Syntax diagram displays can be generated using the Get-Command and Get-Help cmdlets. In this section, we will consider how to interpret the syntax diagrams provided by the cmdlets shown in Table 2 correctly.

ChildItem cmdlets	Item cmdlets	Location cmdlets
Get-ChildItem	Clear-Item	Get-Location
	Copy-Item	Pop-Location
Content cmdlets	Get-Item	Push-Location
Add-Content	Invoke-Item	Set-Location
Clear-Content	Move-Item	
Get-Content	New-Item	PSDrive cmdlets
Set-Content	Remove-Item	Get-PSDrive
	Rename-Item	New-PSDrive
ItemProperty cmdlets	Set-Item	Remove-PSDrive
Clear-ItemProperty		
Copy-ItemProperty	Path cmdlets	
Get-ItemProperty	Join-Path	
Move-ItemProperty	Convert-Path	
New-ItemProperty	Split-Path	
Remove-ItemProperty	Resolve-Path	
Rename-ItemProperty	Test-Path	
Set-ItemProperty		
	PSProvider cmdlets	
	Get-PSProvider	

Table 2: PowerShell Provider cmdlets

The standard method to construct PowerShell commands is through the use of syntax diagrams. A syntax diagram is read starting from the left and ending on the right. The next step is to select an optional parameter and to supply a value for the

44

corresponding placeholder. A command's acceptable form is signified by a syntax diagram paragraph. The PowerShell syntax diagram notation is as follows:

<command-name> -<Required Parameter Name> <Required Parameter Value>

[-<Optional Parameter Name> <Optional Parameter Value>]

[-<Optional Switch Parameters>]

[-<Optional Parameter Name>] <Required Parameter Value>

New-Alias cmdlet commands can be constructed using the following syntax diagram ("About_Command_Syntax - Powershell", 2020):

New-Alias [-Name] <string> [-Value] <string> [-Description <string>]

[-Force] [-Option {None | ReadOnly | Constant | Private | AllScope}]

[-PassThru] [-Scope <string>] [-Confirm] [-WhatIf] [<CommonParameters>]

The Get-Help and Get-Command syntax diagrams are illustrated in capitalized form to enhance readability. PowerShell is, however, not case-sensitive. The elements of a syntax diagram are as follows:

- Command name

- Parameters
- Parameter Values
- Parameters with No Values
- Parameter Sets

In order to understand the command syntax, it is necessary for us to explore each component in detail:

- Command Name

  All PowerShell commands start with the command name, such as Get-Process. In most cases, this is the cmdlet name as well. For example, type Get-ChildItem for the Get-ChildItem command or ls for its alias.

- Parameters

  Command parameters are specific selections that define the command's action. A parameter may require a "value" to be supplied when the command is used. To illustrate, the Get-Command command's Name parameter indicates the target command. The target command is the value for the Name parameter of the Get-Command cmdlet. In commands, parameter names are denoted with a hyphen. To illustrate, when you would like to use the Set-Alias name parameter, type:

  -Name

Parameters are either optional or mandatory. Syntax diagram notation uses parameter names within square brackets ([ ]) to denote optional parameters.

- Parameter Values

A parameter takes on a parameter value. In syntax diagram notation, parameter values are denoted with the parameter value .NET type.

As an example, the Name parameter of the Set-Alias command takes a "string" value, which is a text string. As with most other scripting and programming languages, a string consists of a single word or multiple words enclosed in quotation marks. The Set-Alias Name parameter has a .NET type <String> and would be represented as follows in syntax diagram notation:

[-Name] <string>

In syntax diagram notation, the parameter value .NET type is shown enclosed within angle brackets (< >). The brackets indicate that the .NET type is not a literal but rather a value placeholder. When using the parameter, one uses a .NET type object of the same .NET type as that of the placeholder. To illustrate, specify and supply a value for the name parameter which takes on a "String" .NET type, then type the following:

-Name MyAlias

- Parameters with No Values

Some commands have parameters that do not take any inputs and thus have no parameter values. Such parameters are termed "switch parameters." The name derives from how they behave similar to on/off electrical switches. If switch parameters are included in a command, then they are deemed as switched "on", whereas they are termed switched "off" when not included. In a command, a switch parameter is used by specifying its name preceded by a hyphen.

To illustrate, the Set-Alias cmdlet has a WhatIf switch parameter. This can be switched "on" with the following:

-WhatIf

- Parameter Sets

Command parameter sets list the parameters of a command. Parameter sets typically look like the paragraph of a command syntax diagram. Some cmdlets, like the Set-Alias cmdlet, have a single parameter set, but other cmdlets may have more than one. A parameter set denotes a valid command format. Parameter sets incorporate only parameters which can be suitably used together by the command. Parameters that do not meet this requirement will be included in different sets.

The following are the parameter sets of the Get-Random cmdlet:

Get-Random [[-Maximum] <Object>] [-Minimum <Object>] [-SetSeed <int>]

[<CommonParameters>]

Get-Random [-InputObject] <Object[]> [-Count <int>] [-SetSeed <int>]

[<CommonParameters>]

The first set produces a random value from within a specified range. The range is determined by taking two parameters, Maximum and Minimum. The second set produces a set containing one or more objects from a collection of one or more objects. The object set is supplied using the InputObject parameter. The number of objects is specified using the Count parameter. The remaining parameters in both sets are common parameters and the SetSeed parameter.

The sets show that parameters from the same call can be used together. For example, Count and InputObject can be used together. Analogously, Maximum and Minimum can be used together. However, parameters from different sets, such as Count and Minimum, cannot be used together. PowerShell uses the set indicated by the parameters you submit to the command. In addition, cmdlets have a parameter set that is used by default. This set is used when unique parameters are not submitted. In Get-Random, this is the first set and can be determined by not submitting parameters where the first set is used. The parameter sets also use position order notation. Position order notation is used when parameter values are submitted without specifying the parameter names. In such a scenario, the parameter values will be assigned by PowerShell using type and position.

In summary, parameter sets are a way to further group parameters within the same command. This is particularly useful when you are looking for a specific functionality in a command. In such a setting, the unique parameter in the set indicates the desired functionality.

Symbols in Syntax Diagrams

The first set of items in a syntax diagram are the command name, parameters, and parameter values.

The second set of items are symbols. The following symbols are commonly used:

- Hyphen -: Used to designate the name of the parameter. The hyphen is put before the parameter name without any spaces. To illustrate, for the Set-Alias cmdlet, the name parameter is submitted as follows:

  -Name

- Angle brackets <>: .NET value type of the parameter value. To illustrate, the Set-Alias cmdlet's Name parameter is replaced with a .NET string object. The .NET string object can be one word, or alternatively, more than one word if within quotation marks. To supply a value to the Name parameter of the Set-Alias cmdlet, type the following:

  [-Name] <string>

- Square Brackets [ ]: Signify optional items. The submission of a name for a required parameter may be optional. Alternatively, both the parameter value and the parameter may be optional. Both the Set-Alias cmdlet's Description parameter and its value are optional, because they are within the square brackets. To illustrate, they are depicted like so:

  [-Description <string>]

The brackets may also be used to signify a parameter whose value is required, but whose name is optional. If a parameter's .NET <string> value is required, but its Name specification is optional, then this would be depicted like so:

[-Name] <string>

A parameter can accept one or many values of the .NET type. These are signified by a left and right bracket ([]) affixed to the .NET type. The multiple values can be entered as a comma-separated list.

To illustrate, the Set-Alias cmdlet Name parameter takes a single string while the Get-Process parameter accepts multiple string values. This can be depicted like so for the Set-Alias cmdlet:

Set-Alias [-Name] <string>

Set-Alias -Name MyAlias

And for the Get-Process cmdlet:

Get-Process [-Name] <string[]>

Get-Process -Name Explorer, Winlogon, Services

- Braces {}: Signify an "enumeration". This is a collection of values that are valid for the parameter. These values are split using vertical bars and enclosed with braces. Only one value from the set listed values can be selected.

To illustrate, the Set-Alias cmdlet syntax diagram has an Option parameter with a value enumeration that is like so:

-Option {None | ReadOnly | Constant | Private | AllScope}

This indicates that one of the listed values in the value enumeration can be selected. To illustrate, ReadOnly can be selected like so:

-Option ReadOnly

Optional Items

Square brackets [] are used to surround optional items. To illustrate, in the Set-Alias cmdlet syntax diagram, a set of square brackets surround the Scope parameter and its .NET parameter value placeholder. This is depicted like so:

[-Scope <string>]

Both these examples show a correct use of the Set-Alias cmdlet:

>Set-Alias -Name utd -Value Update-TypeData

>Set-Alias -Name utd -Value Update-TypeData -Scope Global

The parameter value can be required while the parameter name is optional. In the syntax diagram, this is signified by square brackets surrounding only the parameter name. The parameter type is indicated with a placeholder. To illustrate, the syntax diagram for the Set-Alias cmdlet has the following for the Name and Value parameters:

[-Name] <string> [-Value] <string>

All commands in the following sequence use the Set-Alias cmdlet correctly. The results of each all the commands is the same:

>Set-Alias -Name utd -Value Update-TypeData

>Set-Alias -Name utd Update-TypeData

>Set-Alias utd -Value Update-TypeData

>Set-Alias utd Update-TypeData

If the parameter name is omitted in the statement typed, PowerShell tries to use the position of the arguments to assign the values to the parameters. The following is an example of a specification of the Set-Alias command that is not complete:

>Set-Alias utd

When naming and casting to .NET types, square brackets are used. In this setting, square brackets are not being used to signify an optional element.

Aliases

In PowerShell, it is possible to use an alternate name to refer to a cmdlet or command element like a script, file, executable file, or function. This, in PowerShell, is called an alias for that cmdlet or command element. Once created, the alias can be used in place of the PowerShell command or command element. An alias is created by invoking the New-Alias cmdlet. To illustrate, create an alias called "gas" for the cmdlet Get-AuthenticodeSignature by typing this command:

>New-Alias -Name gas -Value Get-AuthenticodeSignature

Once a cmdlet name alias is created, it can be used instead of the name of the cmdlet. To illustrate, to display Authenticode signature information on the SqlScript.ps1 located in the current folder, type:

>Get-AuthenticodeSignature SqlScript.ps1

Or:

>gas SqlScript.ps1

If "word" is created as an alias for Word from Microsoft Office version 11 in your session, then "word" can be typed instead of:

>"C:\Program Files\Microsoft Office\Office11\Winword.exe"

Built-in Aliases

PowerShell has a built-in collection of aliases. Examples include "chdir" and "ls" for the Get-ChildItem and Set-Location cmdlets, respectively.

"dir" is also a built-in alias for the Get-ChildItem cmdlet. To display all computer aliases, including built-in aliases, use the following command:

>Get-Alias

Alias Cmdlets

PowerShell has a set of cmdlets intended for handling aliases. These are:

- Get-Alias: Displays all current session aliases.

- New-Alias: Used for the creation of new aliases.

- Set-Alias: Used for the creation or modification of aliases.

- Export-Alias: Used for exporting aliases to file.

- Import-Alias: Used for importing alias files to PowerShell.

Creating Aliases

To create a new alias, invoke the cmdlet New-Alias. To illustrate, "gh" can be created as an alias for the Get-Help cmdlet by the following:

>New-Alias -Name gh -Value Get-Help

An alias can be included in a command and used with parameters. The two commands below will both display detailed help for the cmdlet GetWmiObject:

>Get-Help Get-WmiObject -Detailed

Or:

>gh Get-WmiObject -Detailed

Saving Aliases

Any created aliases can only be used in that session. To make them available in other sessions or future use, the aliases must be added to the PowerShell profile or exported to file using the cmdlet Export-Alias.

Displaying Aliases

To display all current session aliases, including the ones created during the session, the ones in your profile, and any built-in ones, use the following command:

>Get-Alias

A specific alias can be displayed by using the cmdlet Get-Alias with a Name parameter. To illustrate, any alias starting with "p" will be displayed with the following command:

>Get-Alias -Name p*

The Get-Alias Definition parameter can be used to display the aliases of a specific item. To illustrate, the aliases for the cmdlet Get-ChildItem can be displayed with the command:

>Get-Alias -Definition Get-ChildItem

Get-Alias Output

The Get-Alias cmdlet returns an object called AliasInfo object. The AliasInfo object provides output in a specific format which makes for easy and quick access to the needed information. An alias without a hyphen, such as "ac", will generate an information display that is as follows:

>Get-Alias ac

CommandType   Name

-----------   ----

Alias   ac -> Add-Content

Note that the above format is not usable for aliases that have a hyphen in the alias name.

Aliases and Command Parameters

An alias can be assigned to a command element such as an executable file, cmdlet, function, or script. The assignment, however, cannot occur for a command with specific parameters. To illustrate, the cmdlet Get-EventLog can be assigned an alias, but the cmdlet Get-EventLog with a parameter -LogName and the parameter value System cannot be assigned an alias.

It is possible to create a function with the command and then assign an alias to the function.

Then, when the alias is invoked, the function will invoke the command. Functions will be considered in Chapter Five. A simple function can be created by writing a statement that begins with the function keyword and follows with the function name, with the command enclosed inside braces({}).

To illustrate this process for the cmdlet Get-EventLog with its parameter -LogName and the parameter value System, consider the following statement sequence:

>function Get-SystemEventlog {Get-Eventlog -LogName System}

>Set-Alias   -Name   syslog   -Value   Get-SystemEventlog

The syslog function is an alias to the Get-SystemEventLog function, which contains the desired statement. Hence, when the syslog alias is used, the desired command is invoked.

Alias Objects

Aliases in PowerShell are AliasInfo objects, which are in turn System.Management.Automation.AliasInfo class instances. Since an alias is an object, it can be piped to a cmdlet that can be used to display object information. PowerShell piping will be considered in Chapter Four. The methods and properties for aliases in the current session can be viewed by piping the alias objects obtained by the cmdlet Get-Alias to the cmdlet Get-Member. The command is as follows:

>Get-Alias | Get-Member

The property values of an explicit alias can also be viewed by using piping. The process involves first invoking the Get-Alias cmdlet with the -Name parameter and the name of the alias as the parameter value. Then, the output of the first command is piped to the cmdlet Format-List with parameter Property and value wildcard symbol (*). This pipeline command will display all properties that belong to the alias. The following command illustrates this process for the "dir" alias:

>Get-Alias -Name dir | Format-List -Property *

Alias Provider

PowerShell has a provider for Aliases, or Alias provider. Providers will be considered in Chapter Six. Providers allow you to view specialized data in the same way that data is viewed on a drive in a file system. Aliases can be viewed by using the provider for Aliases. The aliases can be viewed on the Alias: drive which is exposed by the provider for Aliases. The following command takes you into the exposed Alias: drive:

>Set-Location Alias:

This command displays the drive contents:

>Get-ChildItem

This process requires the use of the Set-Location and Get-ChildItem cmdlets, as well as setting the drive as your location. An alternative is to only use the Get-ChildItem cmdlet by setting the Path parameter as the drive. This method is used in PowerShell to view one drive's contents while located in a different one. In this method the Get-ChildItem Path parameter is the name of the drive followed by a colon symbol (:). To illustrate, the command is:

>Get-ChildItem -Path Alias:

Information on a specific alias in the drive (i.e. PowerShell) can be obtained by using the Get-ChildItem cmdlet and the Path parameter. The Path parameter value will be the name of the drive appended with the name of the alias. This method can also be used with the wildcard (*) character for name pattern searches. To illustrate, the aliases in a drive that start with "p" can be displayed with the command:

>Get-ChildItem -Path Alias:p*

Information on the Alias provider can be displayed by using the Get-Help cmdlet as follows:

>Get-Help Alias

Exercises

2.1. How many modules are there in PowerShell 7.0?

2.2. How do cmdlets basically function in PowerShell 7.0?

2.3. Why would writing a cmdlet be useful in PowerShell 7.0?

2.4. What is the main requirement for writing a cmdlet?

2.5. What is the standard naming convention for cmdlets that is used in the Cmdlet Attribute declaration?

2.6. How many provider cmdlets does PowerShell 7.0 have?

2.7. What is the standard and recommended way of constructing PowerShell commands?

2.8. What are aliases used for in PowerShell?

2.9. How many PowerShell 7.0 Alias cmdlets are there and what are their names?

2.10. What cmdlet is used to display the command syntax diagrams of PowerShell cmdlets?

Chapter Summary

The key points of the chapter were:

- Cmdlets are the building blocks for system administration and configuration in the PowerShell environment.

- Cmdlet is a class object that performs actions and usually returns a Microsoft .NET Framework object.

- Cmdlets can be written in C#.

- PowerShell commands can be constructed using syntax diagrams.

- Syntax diagrams are divided into command name, parameters, parameter values, and parameters with no values.

- The Get-Help and Get-Command cmdlets provide a means to display the syntax diagrams of other cmdlets.

- An alias is a nickname for a cmdlet, function, script, file or executable.

In the next chapter you will learn about PowerShell Variables.

Chapter Three:
Variables

Variables

PowerShell variables can be used to store values of all types ("About_Variables - Powershell", 2019). Most importantly, command results, command items, and expression items can all be stored in variables. The specific command and expression items include settings, values, paths, and names. A PowerShell variable is a memory unit that stores values. Variables in PowerShell are denoted by a text string with a preceding dollar sign, denoted as ($). Examples are $my_var, $a, or $process. A variable name can include special characters and spaces. Additionally, variable names are not case-sensitive. Variable names with spaces and special characters, however, are discouraged as they are difficult to script with and their usage can interfere with scripting expression.

PowerShell variables fall into three general categories:

- User-created variables: These are variables the user creates and maintains. These variables, by default, only exist as long as the console window remains open. Upon exiting the console window, these variables are erased. A user-created variable can be saved by adding it to your profile. These variables can also be created in local scripts having a global scope. PowerShell scopes will be considered later in this chapter.

- Automatic variables: These variables are created and maintained by PowerShell. They store the PowerShell state. Their values cannot be changed by users. The variables are changed by PowerShell to preserve their accuracy. An example is the variable $PSHOME, which stores the Powershell installation directory path.

- Preference variables: These are variables that store PowerShell user preferences. PowerShell initially creates them and populates them using default values. Users are then able to alter these values. An example is the variable $MaximumHistoryCount, which defines the maximum entry count in the current session history.

Variable Management

A new PowerShell variable is created by assigning the variable a value by using a statement. It is not necessary to declare the variable beforehand. Variables have a default value of $null. The Get-Variable cmdlet lists all variables in the current session, displayed without the leading dollar symbol ($). To illustrate, these two statements create new variables $NewVariable and $User:

>$NewVariable = 10,20,30

>$User = "User"

The two statements below respectively store the results of the Get-Process command and the formatted output of the Get-Date command:

>$Processes = Get-Process

>$Today = (Get-Date).DateTime

There are two ways to display variable contents. The first method is to type the name of the variable preceded by a leading dollar sign ($). The following two statements show the contents of NewVariable and Today:

>$NewVariable

10

20

30

>$Today

Tuesday, December 12, 05:17:30

The second method is to use the Get-Variable cmdlet with the Name parameter:

>Get-Variable –Name NewVariable

Name   Value

----   -----

NewVariable   {10, 20, 30}

>Get-Variable $Today

Tuesday, December 12, 05:17:30

The value stored in a variable can be changed using another assignment statement. The following statement sequence displays the value of $NewVariable, changes the stored value, and displays $NewVariable again with a new value:

>$NewVariable= 10,20,30

>$NewVariable

10

20

30

>$NewVariable = cat, dog, mouse

>$NewVariable

cat

dog

mouse

The cmdlet Clear-Variable can be used to remove the value stored in a variable. The alternative is to assign the $null value to the variable. The following statements illustrate both these approaches:

>Clear-Variable -Name NewVariable

>$NewVariable

>

>$NewVariable = cat, dog, mouse

>$NewVariable

cat

dog

mouse

>$NewVariable = $null

>$NewVariable

>

The Remove-Variable and Remove-Item cmdlets can be used to delete a variable:

>Remove-Variable -Name NewVariale

>Remove-Item -path Variable:\NewVariable

The second command uses the Variable: drive notation to delete the variable. Variable: drive will be considered later in this chapter.

Types of Variables

PowerShell variables can store an object of any type. The object types can be simple types such as strings, integers, hash tables, and arrays, or they can be more complex, such as objects denoting services, computers, and event logs. Variables in PowerShell are freely typed, meaning that they are not limited to having an explicit object type. One variable can contain an array or a set of un-like object types simultaneously. The variable data type depends on the value .NET types assigned to the variable. The Get-Member cmdlet is used to display the object type of a variable. These concepts are illustrated by the following command sequence:

```
>$a = 12 # System.Int32

> $a

12

>$a = "Word" # System.String

>$a

Word

>[datetime] $dates = "09/12/19"  # This converts
the string to type DateTime object.

>$dates

12 September 2019 12:00:00 AM

>$a =  12, "word"    #array of  System.Int32,
System.String

>$a

12

word
```

>$a = Get-ChildItem C:\Windows # DirectoryInfo and Field Info types

Variable attribute type and casting notation can be used to restrict the object types that can be stored in a variable. This method restricts the object type stored to either an explicitly specified type or a type that PowerShell can convert to the specified type. If the type conversion is not possible, then the statement for the variable assignment fails.

To use this method, denote the specific cast type enclosed in square brackets [] to the left of the variable name in the variable assignment statement (which will include the variable reference symbol ($) on the left or subject side of the statement) with no intervening spaces.

The following command sequence illustration creates three variables: a $numeric variable with a specified type of integer, a "text" variable of specified type string, and a $dates variable of specified type DateTime object.

In case of the $numeric variable:

[int]$numeric = 2

$number = "18"   # In this case the string is converted to an integer.

$number = "Hi"

This will generate the following output:

> [int]$numeric = 2

> $numeric = "18"   # In this case the string is converted to an integer.

> $numeric = "Hi"

Cannot convert value "Hi" to type "System.Int32". Error: "Input string was not in a correct format."

At line:1 char:1

+ $number = "Hi"

+ ~~~~~~~~~~~~~~~~~~

    + CategoryInfo   : MetadataError: (:) [], ArgumentTransformationMetadataException

    + FullyQualifiedErrorId : RuntimeException

In the case of the $words variable:

>[string]$text = "Hello PowerShell"

>$text = 4   # The integer is converted to a string.

>$text += 20   # The plus (+) sign concatenates the strings.

>$text

420

In the case of the $dates variable:

>[datetime] $dates = "12/09/19" # The string is converted to a DateTime object, according to culture setting

> $dates

Monday, December 9, 2019 12:00:00 AM

Variables in Expressions and Commands

Expressions and commands share the same syntax for using variables as previously discussed. The variable name (string) with a leading variable reference dollar ($) symbol is typed in the expression or command. The value that will be used in the expression for the variable depends on how the name of the variable appears in the expression or command. If $variable_name has no other symbols or appears enclosed with a double quotation symbol ("), then the value stored in the variable will be used when the expression or command is evaluated. If $variable_name appears within a single quotation symbol ('), then variable_name will be used when the expression or command is evaluated (note the $ is removed).

The following illustration considers the $PROFILE automatic variable, which stores the path to the file of the user profile, on the console.

>$PROFILE

C:\Users\<User>\Documents\PowerShell\Microsoft.P owerShell_profile.ps1

PS C:\>

In this illustration, PowerShell obtains the value of the $variable, which is an integer value of 1, converts it to text, and concatenates it with 2, where the $variable name is enclosed in double quotation symbol. In the second expression, where the variable name $variable is enclosed in a single quotation symbol, the variable name is converted to text and concatenated with 2.

>[int] $variable = 1

>"$variable" + 2

12

>'$variable' + 2

$variable2

Variable Names with Special Characters

Variable names can include alphanumeric and special characters. The length of the name of the variable is only restricted by the memory available. The recommended practice is for variable names to only include alphanumeric characters as well as the underscore symbol (_). Variable names with spaces and special characters other than the underscore ought to be steered away from because they are hard to use.

Variable names that are designated alphanumeric may contain the following characters:

- Unicode characters contained in categories: Ll, Lm, Ll, Lu, Lo or Nd.

- Underscore symbol (_).

- Question mark (?).

This list contains descriptions for the Unicode categories:

- Ll: LowercaseLetter

- Lm: ModifierLetter

- Ll: LowercaseLetter

- Lu: UppercaseLetter

- Lo: OtherLetter

- Nd: DecimalDigitNumber

The approach for creating or displaying a name for a variable which includes a special character or a space is to enclose the name with curly brace symbols {}. The curly brace symbols are a directive to PowerShell to interpret all characters in the variable name as literals.

Variable names designated as special character may contain any Unicode character other than the following:

1. Right curly brace } character "U+007D".

2. Backtick (`) character "U+0060". The backtick symbol is used by Unicode characters as an escape so they can be considered literals.

PowerShell has a set of reserved variables containing alphanumeric as well as special characters. These variables are variables such as $?,$$,$_ and $^. These are part of the PowerShell set of automatic variables. The following examples illustrate these naming conventions. The curly braces are required because of the (-) special character.

>${list-items} = "a", "b", "c", "d"

>${list-items}

a

b

c

d

>${number-items} = 1,2,3,4,5

>${number-items}

1

2

3

4

5

>${date-items}   =
"01/09/2019","02/09/2019","03/09/2019"

>${date-items}

01/09/2019

02/09/2019

03/09/2019

In this example, a variable called ProgramFiles(x86) with an environmental scope is created and used as an input to the Get-ChildItem cmdlet:

>Get-ChildItem ${env:ProgramFiles(x86)}

The curly braces need to be used to escape the (and) characters. We will discuss the meaning of the env: below when we briefly talk about variable scopes. In order to give a variable a name that includes curly braces, enclose the variable name in braces and use the backtick character to escape the braces in the variable name. To illustrate, the following creates a variable with name array{1} and displays the output:

>${array`{1`}} = "This variable name uses braces and backticks."

>${array`{1`}}

This variable name uses braces and backticks.

Variable Scope

When a variable is created in a particular scope, then it is by default only available in that scope. To illustrate, a variable created within a function only becomes available within that function. A variable created within a script only becomes available within that script. If, however, a script is dot-sourced, then that variable is available in the local or current scope. The default variable scope can be changed using an optional scope modifier. The following variable assignment creates a $Servers variable:

```
>$Global:Servers=
"Server01","Server02","Server03"
```

```
>$Global:Servers
```

Server01

Server02

Server03

This assignment statement is such that the scope of the variable will be global even when created within a function or script.

Access to PowerShell aliases, functions, variables and drives is protected. PowerShell achieves this by limiting the circumstances under which a user can read and modify them. This is facilitated by PowerShell scoping rules. Scoping rules ensure that items are not inadvertently changed when it is not ideal to do so.

The basic scope rules are:

- Scopes are able to nest. Any outer scope is considered the parent scope. Any scopes nested in that parent scope are its child scopes.

- An item created in a scope becomes visible in that scope and any of its child scopes, unless it is explicitly made private. Aliases, variables, functions, or PowerShell drives can be placed in one or multiple scopes.

- An item created within a specific scope can only be modified in that scope, unless a different scope is specified for that purpose.

If an item is created within a scope and has the same name as an item from another scope, then the first item to be created can be hidden under the more recent item, but will not be overridden or modified.

Types of Scopes

PowerShell has the following scopes:

- Global: This is the scope during PowerShell start-up. Variables that are in PowerShell at start-up were created within the global scope. These include preference and automatic variables. This applies analogously to functions. PowerShell user profile aliases, variables, and functions at PowerShell start-up were also created in this scope.

- Local: A current scope. This scope can be global or another scope.

- Script: This is the scope which is generated when a script runs. This is the scope where only the script commands run. This scope is also the current or local scope for the script commands.

It is important to highlight that private is a visibility option for an item rather than a scope. The private option of an item determines whether items outside of its scope can view it.

Parent and Child Scopes

Another scope can be created either by executing a function or script, starting a new session, or a new PowerShell instance. The newly created scope is a nested child scope of the original parent scope. Thus, in PowerShell, scopes are nested child scopes of the parent global scope. It is possible to create multiple scopes and multiple recursive scopes. Items within a parent scope can be used by its child scope unless explicitly made private. The items created and modified within the nested child scope, by default, will not impact the original parent scope. Items in the child scope can affect objects in the parent scope if their scope is specifically specified to be the parent scope when they are created.

Inheritance

A nested child scope will not inherit items such as aliases, variables, and functions from its parent scope. An item of the original parent scope is visible to the nested child scope, unless it is private. These items can be modified by the nested child scope by specifically referencing the original parent scope, however, they are not in the nested child scope. A nested child scope does have a collection of items when it is created. These usually include all aliases with the Option property set to AllScope. The Option property will be discussed later in this chapter under Scope modifiers. This includes all variables with the Option property set to AllScope. Items in a specific scope can be found using the Get-Alias or Get-Variable cmdlets invoked with the target scope as the value for the Scope parameter. To illustrate, variables in the local scope can all be displayed with the command:

>Get-Variable -Scope local

And those in the global scope with the following command:

>Get-Variable -Scope global

Scope Modifiers

A function name or alias may have an optional scope modifier. This can be selected to be one of:

- global: This designates the scope where the name should exist should be Global.

- local: This designates the scope where the name should exist should be Local. The current and local scopes are the same.

- private: This designates the name to be Private and visible only to the local scope.

- script: This designates the scope where the name should exist should be Script. The Script scope is the nearest

- parent of the scope of the script file or Global otherwise.

- using: This allows variables of another scope to be accessed when running scripts using cmdlets like Invoke-Command and Start-Job.

- <variable-namespace>: A scope modifier that is created by a PSDrive provider. The following are examples of the <variable : namespace> syntax:

The script scope is the default script file scope. The local scope is the default aliases scope and default functions scope, even when defined by a script.

81

Using Scope Modifiers

A way to designate the scope when creating a new alias, variable, or function is by using an optional scope modifier. In the case of variables, the syntax is as follows:

>$[<scope-modifier>:]<name> = <value>

In the case of functions, the syntax is as follows:

>function   [<scope-modifier>:]<name> {<function-body>}

This command is an assignment expression to create or modify a variable $a in the local or current scope:

>$a = "a"

To create the variable $a such that it exists in a global scope, use a scope modifier set to global, as follows:

>$global:a = "a"

Similarly, to create the variable $a such that it exists in the script scope, use a scope modifier set to script, as follows:

>$script:a = "a"

The optional scope modifier can be used with functions. This function definition will create a function that exists in the global scope:

>function global:Hello {

```
Write-Host "Hello, World"

}
```

Optional scope modifiers can also be used when denoting a variable within another scope. The following denotes the $variable variable, initially in the current scope and subsequently within the parent global scope:

>$variable

>$global:variable

The Using: Scope Modifier

The Using: scope modifier is a special modifier used to identify a local variable in a remote command. When a modifier is not used, PowerShell requires that variables that are part of remote commands be part of the remote session variable definition. This scope modifier was introduced in Windows PowerShell 3.0.

AllScope Option

An item with an Option property that is AllScope becomes visible to and part of the nested child scope. Modifications to that item in any of the scopes immediately affects all scopes where it is defined.

Managing Scope

A variety of cmdlets also have a parameter that can be used for managing scope. This parameter is called the Scope parameter. This parameter used in conjunction with the cmdlets provides a means to either get, change or create items within a specified scope. This command finds all cmdlet in the session with the Scope parameter:

>Get-Help * -Parameter scope

Variables which are visible within a specific scope can be found using the Get-Variable cmdlet and its Scope parameter. The variables that will be visible include parent scope variables, current scope variables, and global variables. This command displays variables which are visible to the current scope:

>Get-Variable -Scope local

Variables can be created in a scope specific manner using the optional scope modifier or the Set-Variable cmdlet Scope parameter. This command creates a variable with a scope that is global:

>New-Variable -Scope global -Name numeric -Value 1

The New-Alias, Get-Alias or Set-Alias cmdlets have a Scope parameter that can be used for specifying the scope. This command will create an alias whose scope is global:

>New-Alias -Scope global -Name command -Value cmd.exe

It is possible to still display functions within a scope but not use the Scope parameter of a cmdlet. The approach is to first select the target scope and then invoke the cmdlet Get-Item within the target scope.

It is important to note that cmdlets whose parameters include a Scope parameter allow for scopes to be referred to by number. The number labels the relative location of a scope to a different one. Scope 0 is the local or current scope. Scope 1 is the direct parent scope. Scope 2 is the direct parent of Scope 1, and the like. Numbered scopes have great utility in a setting where multiple recursive scopes have been created.

Using Dot Source Notation with Scope

Functions and scripts stick to scope rules. They are created in a specific scope and have an impact only on that scope with the exception being if a parameter of a cmdlet or an optional scope modifier is used to alter the scope. Dot sourcing can also add a function or script to the local scope. When the script executes in the local scope, any aliases, variables and functions created by the script become available to the local scope. A function can be added to the local scope by typing a dot symbol (.) followed by a space preceding the function path location and name within the call to the function. To illustrate, a Sample.ps1 script located in the path C:\Scripts can be executed within its script scope (which is the default scope for a script) with this command:

>C:\Scripts\Sample.ps1

In order to run the Sample.ps1 scripts in the C:\Scripts folder then use any of the following two commands:

>./Sample.ps1

>.\Sample.ps1

This command runs a Sample.ps1 script located in the path C:\Scripts within the current scope (using dot sourcing):

>. C:\Scripts\Sample.ps1

When the call operator, designated with the symbol &, is used to execute a script or function, then it is not included in the local scope. This command executes the Sample.ps1 script in the located in the path C:\Scripts by calling the script via &:

>& C:\Scripts\Sample.ps1

Any variables, functions, or aliases created while executing the Sample.ps1 file will not be available within the local scope.

Restricting Without Scope

Some PowerShell concepts interact with or are comparable to scope. These can be easily mistaken to have the behavior of or similar to scope. Nested prompts, modules, and sessions are not session-nested child scopes of the parent global scope but autonomous environments.

- Sessions

A session can be described as a self-contained environment on which PowerShell operates. When a remote computer-based session is created, PowerShell establishes a persistent connection with that computer. The resulting session is based on this connection, which facilitates the running of several associated commands. The session, being a self-contained environment, has a separate individual scope, but the session is not itself a nested child scope within the session that created it. The session begins with an individual global scope. The original global scope is not dependent on the new global scope of the remote session. Child scopes can be created in the remote session. To illustrate, a script can be executed in the remote session.

- Modules

Modules are used to deliver and share PowerShell tools. A module can be characterized as a component within which aliases, variables, functions, scripts, cmdlets, and other useful items can be contained. Unless specifically stated, module items cannot be accessed externally of the module. A module can, therefore, be added to a session and its public items used without concerns that they will override the functions, scripts, cmdlets, and other items within the session.

Modules are, by default, not loaded into the local scope but rather the highest level of the current PowerShell session's state. This state is either the module session or global session state. When a session is supplemented with a module, this action does not modify the scope of the session. When your scope is global, then module loading will be at the global state. The placement of any exports will be into the tables at the global level. If a module, say module_2, is loaded from within another module, say module_1, then module_2 will be loaded under the state of the session of module_1, rather than the state of the global session. The placement of any exports from module_2 will be into the state of the session of module_1.

In the case where the Import-Module cmdlet has a local Scope parameter, exports will be placed into the object of the local scope instead of at the highest level. If the Import-Module cmdlet with a global value is used within a module to load a different module, then the imported module is loaded with a global state rather than that of the module from which it was imported. The exports of the imported module will analogously load into the state of the global session as well. This feature was designed for a module that could manage other modules. This is used by the PowerShell WindowsCompatibity module to facilitate the loading into the state of the global session loading of proxy modules.

- Nested Prompts

When the user enters a prompt that is nested, this prompt is part of the PowerShell environment in the current scope. Similarly, during script debugging, scripts have a default scope. When a script breakpoint is reached, then the user will go into the script scope. In both cases, the nested prompt is a self-contained environment with no individual scope.

- Private Option

To illustrate, suppose a user first creates a variable with a default scope that is global and additionally has an Option property with a value that is private. If the user proceeds to run a Get-Variable command in a script, then this command will not display the variable. The optional global scope modifier will not display this variable in this setting. The private option of a variable can be set by invoking either the Set-Variable or New-Variable cmdlets with an option parameter. Similarly, the private option of an alias can be set by invoking either the Set-Alias or New-Alias cmdlets with an option parameter.

- Visibility

The Visibility property operates on containers in a similar manner to how the Option property operates on scopes. The Visibility property assumes a value of either Private or Public. Items with a private value can only be changed and viewed by items inside the container that created them. They cannot be changed or viewed when their container is imported or added.

Visibility operates in a different manner within a scope because it is designed for containers. If an item has a private Visibility value within a global scope, then it cannot be changed or viewed in all scopes. If the user tries to change or view the value stored in a variable that has a private Visibility value, this will result in a PowerShell error message.

Let us illustrate these concepts on scope with some examples.

Example: Change a Variable Value Only in a Script

In this illustration, we run a script command to change the stored value inside the variable $ConfirmPrecedence. Initially, display the value stored in the variable $ConformPreference in the current scope using this command:

> $ConfirmPreference

This will yield:

High

Compile the following commands into a script file called Scope.ps1:

$ConfirmPreference = "Low"

"The value of `$ConfirmPreference is $ConfirmPreference."

Execute the script. The script execution alters the stored value in the variable $ConfirmPreference and conveys it within the scope. The resulting output should be similar to the following:

The value of $ConfirmPreference is Low.

The last step is to compare this with the current stored value of the variable $ConfirmPreference within the local scope:

>$ConfirmPreference

This should generate the following output:

High

This illustration demonstrates that modifications to the stored variable value within the scope that is script will have no impact on the stored value of a variable in the global parent scope.

Example: View a Variable Value in Different Scopes

The optional scope modifiers can be used to display the stored variable value in the current scope as well as the parent scope.

Initially, we store a value inside a variable called $test within the scope that is global:

>$test = "Global"

Then, create a script called Sample.ps1. Inside the script place an assignment statement that stores a value in a variable called $test and use an optional scope modifier to state both $test variable versions.

$test = "Local"

"The local value of `$test is $test."

"The global value of `$test is $global:test."

Executing the Sample.ps1 script will generate output that is similar to the following:

The local value of $test is Local.

The global value of $test is Global.

After the script executes, the $test variable value definition in the global scope applies in the local session:

> $test

It will generate the following output:

Global

Example: Change the Value of a Variable in a Parent Scope

A stored variable value can be modified and displayed, unless it is protected by either using a private value for the Option property or a different method, in its parent scope. Initially, assign a stored value to a variable called $test within the scope that is global:

>$test="Global"

Then, create a script file called Sample.ps1. Inside the script, place a variable assignment that stores in a variable called $test and use an optional scope modifier to state both $test variable versions:

$global:test = "Local"

"The global value of `$test is $global:test."

After the script executes, the $test variable value in the global scope is modified:

>$test

This should generate the following output:

Local

Example: Creating a Private Variable

A variable is said to be private if it has a private value for the Option property. Private variables can only be modified or viewed within the scope where they are created, even though they are inherited within the nested child scope. This command assigns a value to a $ptest variable, which is a variable that is private, within the current scope:

>New-Variable -Name ptest -Value 1 -Option private

The $ptest value can be modified and viewed in the current scope:

>$ptest

>$ptest=2

>$ptest

This will yield the following output:

>$test

1

>$ptest = 2

>$ptest

2

Then, create a script called Sample.ps1. Place these commands in the script to view the $ptest value:

"The value of `$Ptest is $Ptest."

"The value of `$Ptest is $global:Ptest."

The resulting output has no value for $ptest because the variable cannot be viewed from the scope of the script:

"The value of $Ptest is ."

"The value of $Ptest is ."

Saving Variables

Variables that are created in a session can only be accessed in that session. They are only part of that session and are removed once the session is closed. Variables can be made available to other PowerShell sessions by adding them to your profile. To illustrate, add this command into your profile to modify the $VerbosePreference variable value in other sessions:

$VerbosePreference = "Continue"

To add a command to your profile, modify the file stored in the path $PROFILE using a text editor.

Variable: drive

The Variable provider exposes the drive designated Variable:. This drive behaves and appears similar to the drive of a file system, but instead contains information about your session variables, such as their values. To change your location to be drive designated Variable:, use this command:

>Set-Location Variable:

The variables and items in the drive designated Variable: can be displayed using the Get-ChildItem or Get-Item cmdlets.

>Get-ChildItem Variable:

A value for a specific variable can be obtained by specifying the drive name and variable name using the notation for a file system. To illustrate, this command displays the value of the $PSCulture variable, which is a PowerShell automatic variable:

>Get-Item Variable:\PSCulture

This will yield the following according to your PowerShell culture setting:

Name	Value
PSCulture	en-US

To display the help file for the drive designated Variable: and its associated provider use this command:

>Get-Help Variable:

Variable Syntax with Provider Paths

The PowerShell variable syntax dollar symbol ($) can also be used with provider paths. The provider path should be prefixed with the dollar symbol ($) to access the provider contents. The provider should, however, implement the interface designated IContentCmdletProvider. The built-in providers supporting this notation are shown in Table 3.

Provider
Environment Provider
Variable Provider
Function Provider
Alias Provider

Table 3: Providers that support variable syntax ($)

Variable Cmdlets

PowerShell has a set of cmdlets that are designed to manage variables. In order to list these cmdlets, type:

>Get-Command -Noun Variable

It will generate the following list:

CommandType	Name	ModuleName
Cmdlet	Clear-Variable	Microsoft.PowerShell.Utility
Cmdlet	Get-Variable	Microsoft.PowerShell.Utility
Cmdlet	New-Variable	Microsoft.PowerShell.Utility
Cmdlet	Remove-Variable	Microsoft.PowerShell.Utility
Cmdlet	Set-Variable	Microsoft.PowerShell.Utility

Help for a certain cmdlet can be displayed with the command:

>Get-Help <cmdlet-name>

Exercises

3.1. What is a variable in PowerShell?

3.2. What is the basic standard PowerShell notation for denoting variables?

3.3. Why should you try to avoid using spaces and special characters in your PowerShell variable names?

3.4. Can a user change a PowerShell Automatic variable?

3.5 Can a user change a PowerShell Preference variable?

3.6. How can a user get a list of all variables in a PowerShell session?

3.7. PowerShell variables are freely typed. What does this statement mean?

3.8. How is the PowerShell variable data type determined?

3.9. How can a user create and denote a PowerShell variable name that has spaces and special characters?

3.10. How is the scope of variables determined?

3.11. How is the PowerShell Variable: drive created, how does it behave and what does it contain?

3.12. How are PowerShell variable cmdlets in a user's session listed?

Chapter Summary

The key points of the chapter were:

- A PowerShell variable is a unit of memory in which values are stored.

- The three general categories of PowerShell variables are user-created variables, automatic variables, and preference variables.

- Cmdlet functioning can be greatly enhanced through the use of variables.

- Variables can be used in commands and expressions.

- Variables are only available in the scope in which they are created.

- Variable constitute an important component of scripting.

In the next chapter you will learn about PowerShell pipelines.

Chapter Four:
Pipelines

Pipelines

In PowerShell, a sequence of commands joined together with pipeline operators is called a pipeline. A pipeline operator is represented by the vertical-bar symbol (|). In the pipeline, each operator transmits the output of the previous command to the following command.

In this arrangement, the results emanating from the first command in the pipeline can be relayed as the input for the following command. This process can be repeated by transmitting the resulting output of this command to another command. The net result is an integrated complex command that can be decomposed into simpler ones. The commands can additionally be arranged into a logical sequence.

In the PowerShell console, the pipeline command is as follows:

> Command-One | Command-Two | Command-Three

In the above illustration, the output objects emitted by Command-One are transmitted to Command-Two. Then, Command-Two performs operations on the input objects and transmits them as inputs to Command-Three. Command-Three similarly performs operations on the input objects and transmits them further into the pipeline. Since there are no further commands in this particular pipeline, the output of Command-Three is displayed on the command-line. In a PowerShell pipeline, commands are executed successively from the left to the right. The overall process is treated as one operation and the results are shown in real-time as they are generated.

Let us consider some simple examples to illustrate the process.

Example : Pipeline to start a Notepad Process and then stop it

This command invokes the Get-Process and Stop-Process cmdlets in a pipeline on a Notepad process object:

>Get-Process notepad | Stop-Process

This pipeline command combines two commands. The first invokes the Get-Process cmdlet with the Name parameter value of notepad to acquire an object that represents a running Notepad process. It then uses the pipeline operator to transmit the object down the pipeline to the cmdlet Stop-Process that stops the process. In the second command, the Stop-Process cmdlet has no parameters such as ID or Name specifying the input process. This is as a result of the process being submitted as part of pipeline input.

Example: Filtering, sorting, and displaying text files in a folder

This example uses the Get-Child-Item cmdlet with the -Path parameter to identify text files in the present location. It then selects the files greater than 100 bytes in length, and uses the Sort-Object cmdlet with the Property parameter to order them based on their lengths. The output shows the sorted files in a formatted table displaying the file lengths and names.

This is performed by the following command:

>Get-ChildItem -Path *.txt |

Where-Object {$_.length -gt 100} |

Sort-Object -Property length |

Format-Table -Property name, length

The pipeline above combines four commands in a stipulated order. This diagram illustrates the pipeline process as well as how the results of a preceding command are transmitted down the pipeline.

Get-ChildItem -Path *.txt

| (FileInfo objects for *.txt)

V

Where-Object {$_.length -gt 100}

| (FileInfo objects for *.txt)

| (Length > 100   )

V

Sort-Object -Property Length

| (FileInfo objects for *.txt)

| (Length > 100)

| (Sorted by length   )

V

Format-Table -Property name, length

| (FileInfo objects for *.txt)

| (Length > 100)

| (Sorted by length   )

| (Formatted in a table)

V

Name	Length
----	------
tmp1.txt	82920
tmp2.txt	114000
tmp3.txt	114000

Using Pipelines

A majority of cmdlets in PowerShell incorporate pipeline support as part of their design. In these cases, it is possible to pipe the output of a cmdlet with a Get noun to the cmdlet of an identical noun. To illustrate, the output of the cmdlet Get-Service can be piped either to the Stop-Service or Start-Service cmdlets.

The following command uses the Get-Service and Start-Service cmdlets in a pipeline to start the service WMI on the local machine:

> Get-Service wmi | Start-Service

Another PowerShell pipeline support feature is that there is a great number of utility cmdlets such as Sort-Object, Where-Object, Group-Object and Get-Member, which are widely used in pipelines. These cmdlets are able to accept all object types as input. Let us look at another example.

Example: Sort Processes on the Computer by Open handles

This illustration, sorts the processes on the local computer by their open handles quantity:

>Get-Process | Sort-Object -Property handles

This will generate the following output (where only the first few lines are shown):

PS C:\> Get-Process | Sort-Object -Property handles

Han dles	NPM (K)	PM(K)	WS(K)	CPU(s)	Id	S I	Process Name
0	16	908	814 0	91.55	96	0	Registry
0	0	52	8		0	0	Idle
0	0	157 6	425 732	6,118 .28	23 76	0	Memory Compre ssion

Another PowerShell pipeline support feature is that objects that are piped can be sent to the export, output, and formatting cmdlets, including Export-CSV, Export-Clixml, Out-File, Format-Table, and Format-List.

Example: List properties for a Process Object

The following illustration uses the cmdlet Format-List to show a property list of an object representing a process.

>Get-Process winlogon | Format-List -Property *

This will generate the following output (where only the first few lines are shown):

PS C:\> Get-Process winlogon | Format-List -Property *

Name   : winlogon

Id   : 46476

PriorityClass   : High

FileVersion   :   10.0.17134.1
(WinBuild.160101.0800)

HandleCount   : 258

WorkingSet   : 8130560

PagedMemorySize   : 2375680

PrivateMemorySize   : 2375680

With practice, you will notice that coalescing simple commands to construct pipelines conserves typing and time while increasing the efficiency of scripting.

Pipeline Processing

In this section, we will look at the manner in which input objects are processed in pipeline execution and bound to the parameters of cmdlets.

Accepts pipeline input

To illustrate, the following command helps to identify if there are any Start-Service cmdlet parameters that accept inputs from a pipeline:

> Get-Help Start-Service -Full

Alternatively, you can display the parameter section of the help file on the Start-Service cmdlet with the following command:

>Get-Help Start-Service -Parameter *

In this output excerpt shown below, the important sections for our purposes are highlighted in **bold**:

PS C:\> Get-Help Start-Service -Parameter *

-InputObject <ServiceController[]>

Specifies ServiceController objects representing the services to be started. Enter a variable that contains the objects, or type a command or expression that gets the objects.

Required?	true
Position?	0
Default value	None
Accept pipeline input?	**True (ByValue)**
Accept wildcard characters?	false

-Name <String[]>

Specifies the service names for the service to be started.

The parameter name is optional. You can use Name or its alias, ServiceName , or you can omit the parameter name.

Required?   true

Position?   0

Default value   None

Accept pipeline input?   True (ByPropertyName, ByValue)

Accept wildcard characters? false

The displayed help file for the cmdlet Start-Service indicates that only the parameters Name and InputObject can accept input from a pipeline. When objects are sent through a pipeline to the Start-Service cmdlet, PowerShell tries to couple the input objects with the Name and InputObject parameters.

Cmdlet parameters are able to accept inputs from a pipeline in one of the following ways:

- ByValue: The parameter is able to accept values matching the anticipated .NET type or alternatively, able to convert to the anticipated type. To illustrate, the Start-Service Name parameter is able to accept input from a pipeline by value. It is able to accept objects that are strings or objects that can be transformed into strings.

- ByPropertyName: The parameter is able to accept input from a pipeline only if the input object owns a property whose name is the same as that of the parameter. To illustrate, the Start-Service Name parameter is able to accept objects that are input with a property that is called Name. In order to determine the properties that an object has, it may be piped to the Get-Member cmdlet.

Some cmdlet parameters are able to accept objects that are input using both property name or value parameters, which makes it less difficult to accept pipeline input.

Parameter Binding

In a pipeline, when objects are being piped from one command to another, PowerShell attempts to associate the piped objects with a parameter of the receiving cmdlet. The parameter binding component of PowerShell associates the input objects with cmdlet parameters according to the following criteria:

- The parameter is able to accept a pipeline input.

- The parameter is able to accept the object type that is sent, or alternatively, a type that may be transformed to the specified type.

109

- The parameter is not one of the parameters utilized within the command.

To illustrate, the cmdlet Start-Service holds a number of parameters; however, only two of these, InputObject and Name, are able to accept input from a pipeline. The parameter InputObject accepts service objects and the parameter Name accepts strings. It is, therefore, possible to pipe service objects, strings, and objects that have properties that may be transformed to service objects or string.

PowerShell looks to manage the parameter binding process as effectively as possible. It is not possible to force or suggest that PowerShell should bind with a given parameter. The command will fail if PowerShell is unable to bind the objects that are piped.

One-at-a-time processing

When objects are piped to a receiving command, the process is similar to using a command parameter for submitting the objects.

Let us illustrate these concepts with a simple example.

Example: Display a table of service objects

In this illustration, the pipeline is used to present a service object table. The pipeline is as follows:

>Get-Service | Format-Table -Property Name, DependentServices

The first few lines of the output generated are as follows:

PS C:\> Get-Service | Format-Table -Property Name, DependentServices

Name	DependentServices
----	-----------------
AbtSvcHost	{}
AdobeARMservice	{}
AdobeFlashPlayerUpdateSvc	{}
AJRouter	{}
ALG	{}
AppIDSvc	{applockerfltr}
Appinfo	{}
AppMgmt	{}
AppReadiness	{}
AppVClient	{}

In a practical sense, the output is similar to one produced with the Format-Table cmdlet parameter InputOject, which formats a set of objects. To illustrate, the set of services can be saved in a variable to be submitted using the parameter InputObject. In order to illustrate this, let us consider the following commands:

>$services = Get-Service

>Format-Table -InputObject $services -Property Name, DependentServices

This sequence will generate the following output (where only the first few lines are shown):

PS C:\> $services = Get-Service

PS C:\> Format-Table -InputObject $services - Property Name, DependentServices

Name	DependentServices
AbtSvcHost	{}
AdobeARMservice	{}
AdobeFlashPlayerUpdateSvc	{}
AJRouter	{}
ALG	{}
AppIDSvc	{applockerfltr}
Appinfo	{}
AppMgmt	{}
AppReadiness	{}

AppVClient	{}
AppXSvc	{}
AssignedAccessManagerSvc	{}

Notice how the outputs are essentially the same. You can think of the pipeline as a "shorthand" method for the longer, more explicit method called above.

Alternatively, the command may be embedded in the parameter InputObject:

>Format-Table -InputObject (Get-Service) -Property Name, DependentServices

This will generate the following output (where only the first few lines are shown):

PS C:\> Format-Table -InputObject (Get-Service) -Property Name, DependentServices

Name	DependentServices
----	-----------------
AbtSvcHost	{}
AdobeARMservice	{}
AdobeFlashPlayerUpdateSvc	{}
AJRouter	{}
ALG	{}
AppIDSvc	{applockerfltr}

113

In this arrangement there is a critical difference. In a pipeline, when multiple objects are piped to a receiving command, PowerShell sends the objects one a time. But when the command parameter is used, these objects are transmitted as a simgular array object. The difference may be minor but its effects are substantial. When a pipeline is executed, PowerShell will enumerate any type implementing the interface IEnumerable and then send members one at a time across the pipeline. The exception to this approach is [hashtable], which needs a GetEnumerator() method call.

In these examples, a hashtable and an array are pipe inputs of the cmdlet Measure-Object. The purpose of the setup is to count, in each case, the number of input objects the cmdlet receives in the pipeline. Both the hashtable and the array have multiple members. Only the pipeline involving the array results in a one at a time enumeration.

In PowerShell, the following command:

>@(1,2,3) | Measure-Object

will generate:

Count   : 3

Average :

Sum   :

Maximum :

Minimum :

Property :

and the following command:

>@{"One"=1;"Two"=2} | Measure-Object

will generate:

Count   : 1

Average :

Sum   :

Maximum :

Minimum :

Property :

In a similar manner, if multiple process objects are piped from the cmdlet Get-Process to the cmdlet Get-Member, PowerShell will send each of the process objects, one at a time, to the Get-Member cmdlet. The Get-Member cmdlet will show two types of input. The first is the input process objects' .NET type. The second is their methods and properties. The command is as follows:

>Get-Process | Get-Member

This call will generate the following output (where only the first few lines are shown):

TypeName: System.Diagnostics.Process

Name	MemberType	Definition
Handles Handlecount	AliasProperty	Handles =
Name ProcessName	AliasProperty	Name =
NPM NonpagedSystemMemorySize64	AliasProperty	NPM =
PM PagedMemorySize64	AliasProperty	PM =

It is important to note that, in the above output, the Get-Member cmdlet eliminates any duplicates. Hence, if all the objects are of one type, then only this object type is displayed. If we use the parameter embedding method, which embeds the process in the InputObject parameter, with the following command:

>Get-Member -InputObject (Get-Process)

it will generate the following output (where only the first few lines are shown):

PS C:\> Get-Member -InputObject (Get-Process)

TypeName: System.Object[]

Name	MemberType	Definition
Count	AliasProperty	Count = Length

Add   Method   int
IList.Add(System.Object value)

Address   Method   System.Object&,
mscorlib,   Version=4.0.0.0,   Culture=neutral,
PublicKeyToken=b77a5c561934e089 Address(int)

Clear   Method   void
IList.Clear()

If, on the other hand, the Get-Member InputOject parameter is used, then it receives System.Diagnostics.Process objects as an array as well as one unit. It shows the properties of the objects based on an array. This is illustrated by the array symbol [] following the type name of the System.Object.

This output result may not match what was intended. If, however, the mismatch is understood or expected, then it may still be useful for the purpose at hand. To illustrate, there is a Count property that can be used by array objects. This can be used to obtain a number count of the running computer processes. This can be done with the following command:

>(Get-Process).count

The important takeaway from these examples is that objects transmitted down a pipeline are supplied one at each time.

Line Continuation

The PowerShell has a pipeline support feature that enhances the readability of pipelines. This feature allows the pipeline to split across many lines. If the last entry on a line is the pipe operator symbol (|), then PowerShell will join the two lines through its parser so the current command may continue constructing the pipeline.

As an example, consider the following pipeline command:

>Command-One | Command-Two | Command-Three

One can write this line as:

>Command-1 |

  Command-2 |

    Command-3

The resulting leading spaces on subsequent lines have no impact. This indentation format is desirable because it enhances the readability. PowerShell 7.0 has extra support for pipeline continuation by allowing the pipeline operator symbol (|) to be placed when the line starts.

The following two illustrative templates show how to use this new functionality when constructing a PowerShell pipeline command:

Wrapping with a pipe at the beginning of a line (no backtick required)

Get-Process | Where-Object CPU | Where-Object Path

  | Get-Item | Where-Object FullName -match "AppData"

  | Sort-Object FullName -Unique

Wrapping with a pipe on a line by itself

Get-Process | Where-Object CPU | Where-Object Path

  |

  Get-Item | Where-Object FullName -match "AppData"

  |

  Sort-Object FullName -Unique

It is important to note that when working with these illustrative templates in the console, code containing pipelines should be pasted at the start of the console line using only CTRL+V rather than right-clicking a mouse and pasting from the drop-down menu. CTRL+V will submit the entirety of the code, whereas right-clicking will submit the input line by line. The new templates, in turn, allow for lines to terminate without a vertical bar symbol (|). In this scenario, PowerShell will interpret the input as complete if a line terminates without a vertical bar symbol when submitted line by line and execute the line.

Exercises

4.1. How are PowerShell commands connected to form a pipeline?

4.2. In what order are two connected commands in a pipeline processed?

4.3. How is object processing handled in a pipeline operation?

4.4. What are the two ways in which cmdlet parameters can accept pipeline input in a pipeline?

4.5. What are PowerShell's parameter binding component's criteria for associating pipeline input objects with cmdlet parameters?

4.6. How does PowerShell pipe multiple objects to a command in a pipeline?

Chapter Summary

The key points of the chapter were:

- A PowerShell pipeline is a series of commands connected by a pipeline operator.

- Pipelines allow commands to be combined in order to create more powerful commands.

- PowerShell has features that make designing and using pipelines a useful scripting function.

- Pipelines make scripting more efficient.

In the next chapter you will learn about functions.

Chapter Five:
Functions

Functions

A function constitutes a list of statements with a user-assigned name. The function can be executed by typing its name. The statements included within the list will execute as if they had been typed on the console.

A function may be simple, such as :

>function Get-PowerShellProcess { Get-Process PowerShell }

A function may also be more complex. It may have the complexity of an application or a cmdlet. Functions, similar to cmdlets, may contain parameters as well. These parameters may be positional, named, dynamic, or switch.

Either a pipeline or console can read a function. Functions can be constructed to return values, which can be shown. These values can also be made part of variable assignments passed to cmdlets or other functions. A function can have a particular return value specified through the keyword return. This keyword will not suppress or affect other output designated to be returned from the function. However, using return will trigger an exit from the function on that line.

A function can have separate statement lists categorised by the keywords Process, Begin, and End. These three types of statement lists have distinct methods for handling pipeline input. A filter is a particular class of functions designated with the keyword Filter. Functions can also be constructed to behave or operate similar to cmdlets without requiring C# programming.

Function Syntax

The syntax for specifying a function is as follows:

function   [<scope:>]<name>
[([type]$parameter1[,[type]$parameter2])]

```
{
  param([type]$parameter1 [,[type]$parameter2])

  dynamicparam {<statement list>}

  begin {<statement list>}

  process {<statement list>}

  end {<statement list>}
}
```

A function has the following components:

- List of PowerShell statements demarcated with brace symbols {}

- Function keyword

- Scope which is optional

- User selected name

- Named parameters which are optional

Simple Functions

A simple function is simply a standard function deployed without the optional components (named parameters and a scope modifier).

A simple function syntax is as follows:

function <function-name> {statements}

To illustrate, this function starts PowerShell in Administrator mode:

function   Start-PSAdmin   {Start-Process PowerShell -Verb RunAs}

The function can be used by invoking it with its name:

>Start-PSAdmin

Statements can be added to a function by typing different statements on separate lines, or by demarcation with the semicolon symbol (;). At this stage, it would be informative to illustrate the concepts with a simple example.

Example: A function for finding .jpg files that were changed after a specific date

This function identifies all files with extension .jpg located in the path $env:UserProfile changed after the date specified by the $Start variable:

```
function Get-NewPix

{

  $start = Get-Date -Month 1 -Day 1 -Year 2010

  $allpix    =    Get-ChildItem    -Path
$env:UserProfile\*.jpg -Recurse

    $allpix | Where-Object {$_.LastWriteTime -gt
$Start}

}
```

Convenient functions can be organized into a toolbox and added into your profile.

Function Names

Functions may have any name assigned to them. The best practice recommendation, however, is for the names to conform to established standard PowerShell naming conventions for all commands. These conventions include a recommendation that the names comprise a pairing of a verb and a noun. In doing so, the noun characterizes the item the function acts on, and the verb describes the function's action. The verb should be one of the approved PowerShell standard verbs for commands. Standard verbs help keep the names of all commands coherent, straightforward, and obvious to users.

Functions Parameters

Named Parameters

A function can define named parameters of an arbitrary number. The named parameters have an assigned default value. Parameters can be defined inside or outside the function brace symbols { }. When defined within the brace symbols, a Param keyword must be used. The syntax is as follows:

function <name> {

param ([type]$parameter1[,[type]$parameter2])

<statement list>

}

When parameters are defined outside the brace symbols, then the required internal brace Param keyword may be omitted. The syntax is as follows:

function <name> [([type]$parameter1[,[type]$parameter2])] {

<statement list>

}

To illustrate, the external brace syntax may be used as follows:

>Function Add-Numbers($one, $two) {

$one + $two

}

126

The internal brace approach is the preferred method, but either approach will give the desired result. When the function is executed, the supplied parameter value is assigned to each variable that contains the name of the parameter. The variable value may be used inside the function.

Let us consider a simple example to illustrate these concepts.

Example: Get-SmallFiles function

In this illustration, a function named Get-SmallFiles is defined. The function includes a parameter called $Size. The function shows all files smaller than a user than the $Size parameter value, and does not include directories:

```
function Get-SmallFiles {
  Param($Size)
  Get-ChildItem $HOME | Where-Object {
    $_.Length -lt $Size -and !$_.PSIsContainer
  }
}
```

Inside the function, the variable called $Size, which matches the defined parameter name, can be used. The function can be used with this command

```
>Get-SmallFiles -Size 50
```

127

A value can be passed to the named parameter without referring to its name. To illustrate, this command produces identical results to the command above:

> Get-SmallFiles 50

A parameter can have an assigned default value. The default value can be defined using a definition expression. The definition expression involves placing an equal sign = to the right of the parameter followed by the default value. This is illustrated in the following revised Get-SmallFiles function definition:

```
function Get-SmallFiles ($Size = 100) {

  Get-ChildItem $HOME | Where-Object {

    $_.Length -lt $Size -and !$_.PSIsContainer

  }

}
```

If Get-SmallFiles is typed with the value omitted, the function will assign a 100 value to $Size. If, on the other hand, a value is supplied, the function will be evaluated with the supplied value. The other option is to attach a help string describing the parameter default value. This is done by first attaching a PSDefaultValue attribute to the parameter description. The second step is to specify the PSDefaultValue Help property of the attached attribute. This example shows how to provide a brief help string describing the specified default value for the Size parameter of the function Get-SmallFiles,by attaching a PSDefaultValue attribute:

```
function Get-SmallFiles {
  param (
    [PSDefaultValue(Help = '100')]
    $size = 100
  )
}
```

Positional Parameters

A function parameter that does not have a name assigned to it is called a positional parameter.

PowerShell assigns values to positional parameters by using the order of the supplied function's parameter values. The values for the positional parameters are assigned to a variable called $args, which is an array type, and ordered to match with the function's parameter values. To illustrate, the first value supplied after the name of the function is assigned a value on the first of the positions in $args, $args[0].

The Get-Extension function in this illustration attaches a file name .txt extension to a supplied file name positional parameter:

```
>function Get-Extension {
```

```
$name = $args[0] + ".txt"

$name

}
```

The output that is obtained when the function is invoked in the command line is as follows:

```
>function Get-Extension {

$name = $args[0] + ".txt"

$name

}

>Get-Extension myTextFile
```

is:

myTextFile.txt

Switch Parameters

A function parameter that has a name but not a required value is called a switch parameter. The parameter is supplied to the function by using only its name. The switch parameter is defined by specifying its type as [switch] before its name in the function definition, as shown in the following illustration:

```
>function Switch-Item {

param ([switch]$on)

if ($on) { "Switch on" }

else { "Switch off" }
```

}

When the switch parameter name occurs after the name of the function, the function will show a "Switch on" signal. If the name of the switch parameter is not supplied, however, then the function will show a "Switch off" signal. These concepts are illustrated in the following command sequence:

```
>function Switch-Item {

  param ([switch]$on)

  if ($on) { "Switch on" }

  else { "Switch off" }

}
>Switch-Item -on

Switch on

>Switch-Item

Switch off
```

The switch parameter can also be supplied to the function using Boolean value notation. This is illustrated in the following command sequence:

```
>Switch-Item -on:$true

Switch on

>Switch-Item -on:$false

Switch off
```

Functions and Pipeline Objects

Any function has the ability to take a pipeline input. In this input, the Process, Begin, and End keywords control how the function handles the processing of the pipeline. The following syntax illustrates how these three keywords are used:

```
function <name> {

  begin {<statement list>}

  process {<statement list>}

  end {<statement list>}

}
```

The statement list following the Begin keyword runs only once at the start of the function evaluation. It is important to note that when the Process, Begin, and End keyword blocks are used, all function code has to be contained within those blocks. As long as one of these blocks is defined, any code that resides outside of the blocks will not be recognized or executed.

The statement list bound to the Process keyword runs once for each pipeline input object. While this block is executing, each of the objects of the pipeline will be allocated, one object at a time, to the variable $\_$, which is an automatic variable. When all the pipeline objects have been received by the function, then the statement list with the keyword End runs once.

If no Process, Begin, or End keywords are found in the function definition, then PowerShell treats all function statements collectively as that of an End block statement list.

The following function uses only the Process keyword. The function shows output from a sample pipeline:

```
>function Get-Pipeline
{
  process {"The value is: $_"}
}
```

This properties of this function can be demonstrated using the following command, which enters a comma-separated list of numbers as the pipeline input:

```
>1,2,4 | Get-Pipeline
The value is: 1
The value is: 2
The value is: 4
```

When a function is used within a pipeline, the pipeline input objects of the function are allocated to the variable $input, which is an automatic variable. The function will run all statements within the Begin block before any of the pipeline objects are sent to the function. The function will run all statements within the End block after all pipeline input objects have been received.

The following example illustrates the properties of the automatic $input variable for a function using a Begin keyword and an End keyword. The function Get-PipelineBeginEnd is defined as follows:

>function Get-PipelineBeginEnd

{

  begin {"Begin: The input is $input"}

  end {"End: The input is $input" }

}

This command and its resulting output illustrates how the function processes a pipeline input:

>1,2,4 | Get-PipelineBeginEnd

Begin: The input is

End: The input is 1 2 4

In the case that the Process keyword is additionally used in the function definition, then each pipeline input object is removed from the $input variable and allocated to $_. The following function has a Process keyword in its definition:

function Get-PipelineInput

```
{
  process {"Processing:  $_ " }
  end {"End:   The input is: $input" }
}
```

In this illustration, each function pipeline input object is sent for processing by the Process keyword statement block after it is piped. The Process keyword statements will run a single object at a time. The automatic $input variable will be empty when the evaluation of the function arrives on the End block evaluation. This is demonstrated by the following output:

>1,2,4 | Get-PipelineInput

Processing: 1

Processing: 2

Processing: 4

End: The input is:

Filters

A function type that is specifically designed to run each pipeline object is called a filter. A filter is similar to a function that has only a Process{<statement list>} block. The following shows the filter syntax:

filter [<scope:>]<name> {<statement list>}

135

The example filter below collects log entries from a running pipeline and then shows only either the entry message portion or the whole entry:

```
filter Get-ErrorLog ([switch]$message)

{

if ($message) { Out-Host -InputObject
$_.Message }

else { $_ }

}
```

Function Scope

A function only exists within the scope which it is created. If a script creates a function, then all statements within the script can access the function. A function created by a script cannot be accessed from within the console by default. The function scope can additionally be specified. To illustrate, the function below shows had to add a function to a global scope:

```
function global:Get-DependentSvs {

Get-Service | Where-Object
{$_.DependentServices}

}
```

A function that has a global scope can be used at the console, in other functions, and in scripts. In general, each function creates a function scope. The items created within the function, such as variables, exist only within that function's scope.

A function variable cannot, however, be called outside the function scope even if the function itself is within the global scope. This scenario is illustrated by the following command sequence and output:

```
function global:Send-Greeting {
    [CmdletBinding()]
    Param(
        [Parameter(Mandatory=$true)]
        [string] $Name
    )
    Process
    {
        Write-Host ("Hello " + $Name + "!")
    }
}
>Send-Greeting –Name user
Hello user!
>$Name
>
```

Function: Drive

All PowerShell filters and functions are stored automatically within the drive called Function:. The Function provider in PowerShell exposes this drive. The way to refer to this drive is to type a colon symbol (:) after the word Function, similar to a file system drive. This command shows all current session functions:

>Get-ChildItem function:

More information about the Function: drive is available from the function provider help topic accessed by typing Get-Help Function. The function statement list is specified in the function definition according to the function syntax. To illustrate, to show the commands of the PowerShell built-in Help function, enter the following command:

>(Get-ChildItem function:help).Definition

An alternative syntax is shown below:

>$function:help

Reusing Functions

Functions created in a session are only available for use in that particular session. Once the session is closed, the function is no longer available and calling the function in a new session will return an error. However, a function can be made universally available in any current or future session by adding the function to your profile or saving it to a script file.

Consider below the following function called Get-CmdletAlias, which obtains the alias of every cmdlet:

```
function Get-CmdletAlias ($cmdletname) {

 Get-Alias |

    Where-Object -FilterScript {$_.Definition -like "$cmdletname"} |

       Format-Table -Property Definition, Name -AutoSize

  }
```

One useful PowerShell profile is the "all users for all hosts" profile accessed by either locating the $PSHOME\Profile.ps1 file or entering the following script, $env:windir\System32\PowerShell\v1.0\Profile.ps1, in PowerShell. To save a function for future use, next enter the function in the script file. In doing so, the function can be invoked in all PowerShell session sessions. This scenario is demonstrated as follows, using the Get-Command cmdlet example from above:

```
>Get-CmdletAlias Get-Command

Definition  Name

----------  ----
```

Get-Command gcm

The function may also be saved in a script file, such as AliasFunction.ps1, located in the folder <path>. Then, invoking the following command will bring the function into the current session as needed:

<path>\AliasFunction.ps1

Function Help

The help file for cmdlets, scripts, providers, and functions can be displayed by calling the cmdlet Get-Help. The Get-Help cmdlet invoked with the name of the function supplied for the Name parameter gets help for the specified function. To illustrate, to show the help file for the function Get-MyDisks using the Get-Help cmdlet, enter this command:

>Get-Help Get-MyDisks

Help for a function can be written by making use of either of the following methods:

• Comment-Based function help: Use comment-based special keywords to create a topic in the function help file. The help comments may be placed in one of four locations. These are the lines before the keyword function, outside the function braces, after the right brace of the statement list, or outside the function braces before the left brace of the statement list. We will discuss the syntax in further detail in a later section.

- XML-Based function help: This type of help is similar to that of cmdlets. This type of help is required in help-topic localization for multiple languages and is created using the .ExternalHelp version of the comment-based help special keyword within the comments.

Comment-Based Help Syntax

Comment-based function help, which has an identical format to that produced using XML files, is viewed by invoking the Get-Help cmdlet and using any of its parameters.

The general comment-based help syntax is as follows:

```
<#

.<help keyword>

<help content>

#>
```

or:

```
.<help keyword>

<help content>
```

Comment-based help may take the form of a single-line comment or a sequence of comments. To add a multi-line comment, enclose the comment block within <# and #>. Alternatively, precede each comment line with the comment symbol (#). In such an arrangement, PowerShell will interpret all #'d block lines as comments.

Help topic comment-based lines must be neighboring. In other words, there must be one or more empty lines separating the final comment line of the non-help comment topic and the first line of the comment-based help topic.

Comment-based help sections are defined using keywords. A dot symbol (.) must precede a keyword within the comment-based help. The order of the keywords may be arbitrary, and the names of the keywords are not case-sensitive. To illustrate, a function description is preceded by the keyword "Description" as follows:

```
<#
```

.Description

Get-Function displays the name and syntax of all functions in the session.

```
#>
```

One or more keywords are required in a comment block. A comment block may have the same keyword appearing multiple times, such as "EXAMPLE". The keyword-designated help content may range many lines and starts on the subsequent line to the keyword.

The function comment-based help may be placed in a single location from a choice of the following three:

- Preceding the keyword used for functions. Only a single line that is blank is permitted between the keyword for the function and the final function help line.

- When the body of the function concludes

- When the body of the function starts

To illustrate:

```
<#

.<help keyword>

<help content>

#>

function Get-Function { }
```

or:

```
function Get-Function

{

  # function logic

<#

.<help keyword>

<help content>

#>
```

}

or:

```
function Get-Function
{
<#
.<help keyword>
<help content>
#>
  # function logic
}
```

are all appropriate templates for creating a comment-based function help topic.

Exercises

5.1. How does PowerShell run function commands?

5.2. Can functions have parameters? If so, what types?

5.3. Where are the two places where function parameters can be read?

5.4. What are the components of a function?

5.5. What types of functions can accept input from a pipeline?

5.6. What is the scoping rule for functions?

5.7. What does the Function: drive do?

Chapter Summary

The key points of this chapter were:

- A function is a list of statements with a user assigned name.

- Functions should have names that follow PowerShell naming conventions.

- Parameters may be used with functions.

- Filters are a type of function that runs on each of the objects in a pipeline.

- Functions can be enhanced through the creation comment-based or XML-based help.

In the next chapter you will learn about modules and providers.

Chapter Six:
Modules and Providers

In this chapter we will consider modules and providers. Modules and providers are environment customization constructs that enhance the functioning of PowerShell. Modules may be used to provide access to more PowerShell commands while providers allow for enhanced access to data in a specialized data store.

In the first part of this chapter we will look at modules, and the second part, we will look at providers.

Modules

In this section, we explore PowerShell modules. In PowerShell a unit that holds commands is called a module. The commands may be functions, variables, aliases, cmdlets, and providers. All providers and cmdlets in a PowerShell session are delivered by a snap-in or a module. Administrators who receive modules can add the commands in the modules to their PowerShell sessions and use them just as they would use the built-in commands. Command authors may use modules to arrange commands and deliver them to others.

PowerShell users can obtain modules, introduce the commands contained in the modules to their sessions, and supplement the built-in commands available to them.

Module Auto-Loading

Introduced in Windows PowerShell 3.0, an automatic module import occurs whenever a command contained within an installed module is called an initial time in a session. This reduces the amount of profile configuration, environment set-up, and module management before module commands can be available for use. Module commands can be located more easily. This feature also be used with the increased functionality introduced to cmdlets like Get-Command, which are able to obtain commands directly from installed modules. This allows for a command to be found and used without the need for module importing.

The following commands show how this feature could prompted using the Get-Content cmdlet:

- Running the command:

>Get-Content -Path C:\Test\Text.txt

- Getting the command:

>Get-Command Get-Content

- Displaying the command help:

>Get-Help Get-Content

This feature considers Get-Command calls, including the wildcard symbol (*), to be exploratory rather than for use. This feature only applies to modules located in the path stored in the PSModulePath variable. Modules not in this location require an import using the cmdlet Import-Module. The second example, where this feature does not apply, are commands that make use of PowerShell providers. This feature can be further configured using the $PSModuleAutoloadingPreference variable.

For example, the use of a command that requires the WSMan: drive, such as the Get-PSSessionConfiguration cmdlet, might require that you run the Import-Module cmdlet to import the Microsoft.WSMan.Management module, as this module includes the WSMan:drive. It may still be required that you run the Import-Module command to import a module and use the $PSModuleAutoloadingPreference variable to enable, disable, and configure automatic importing of modules.

Using a Module

Using a module requires three tasks:

1. Module installation.

2. Find commands added by the module.

3. Use commands added by the module.

In this chapter we consider how to perform these tasks alongside other useful information for module management.

Module Installation

PowerShell has a set of pre-installed modules. The following statements explain the steps to install a module on the local machine.

First, create a current user Modules directory. This may be performed with the following command, which makes use of the New-Item cmdlet:

>New-item   -Type   Directory   -Path $HOME\Test\WindowsPowerShell\Modules

Copy the module folder (called C:\ps-test\MyModule in this illustration) to the Modules folder. This may be performed by using the following command, which uses the Copy-Item cmdlet:

>Copy-Item   -Path   C:\ps-test\MyModule   -Destination `

$HOME\Documents\WindowsPowerShell\Mo dules

Modules may be installed in any arbitrary location, but housing modules within a default location make for easier module management.

Finding Installed Modules

Modules that are installed within a default location, but have not been imported into the session, can be found with this command:

>Get-Module -ListAvailable

Modules that have been imported into the session can be found using this command:

>Get-Module

Finding Module Commands

Available module commands can be found using the cmdlet Get-Command. The cmdlet Get-Command parameters can be used to filter commands by noun, name, or module. The following command finds module commands:

>Get-Command -Module <module-name>

To illustrate, this command finds commands within the module BitsTransfer:

>Get-Command -Module BitsTransfer

It will generate the following output:

PS C:\> Get-Command -Module BitsTransfer

CommandType	Name	Version	Source
Cmdlet	Add-	2.0.0.0	BitsTransfer

BitsFile

Cmdlet	Complete-BitsTransfer	2.0.0.0	BitsTransfer
Cmdlet	Get-BitsTransfer	2.0.0.0	BitsTransfer
Cmdlet	Remove-BitsTransfer	2.0.0.0	BitsTransfer
Cmdlet	Resume-BitsTransfer	2.0.0.0	BitsTransfer
Cmdlet	Set-BitsTransfer	2.0.0.0	BitsTransfer
Cmdlet	Start-BitsTransfer	2.0.0.0	BitsTransfer
Cmdlet	Suspend-BitsTransfer	2.0.0.0	BitsTransfer

Getting Help for Module Commands

Modules may contain Help files for exported commands contained within them. The cmdlet Get-Help will show command help topics. Starting with

Windows PowerShell 3.0, the module Help files and their associated updates may be downloaded. This command obtains help for module commands:

>Get-Help <command-name>

This command obtains online help for module commands:

>Get-Help <command-name> -Online

This command downloads and installs module command help files:

>Update-Help -Module <module-name>

Importing a Module

Importing a module involves introducing a module file or module into the session environment. This is required when the module is not located or installed in paths specified within the variable $env:PSModulePath. Alternatively, importing is needed when the module is not housed in a folder but is rather in file form such as .psm1 or .dll.

You also might choose module importing to use Import-Module command parameters, such as the parameter Prefix, which attaches a specified prefix to noun names of the commands imported. Alternatively, you can use the cmdlet Import-Module parameter NoClobber to prevent the addition of commands that may replace the existing session commands.

The cmdlet Import-Module is used for importing modules. Current session module imports from the location path PSModulePath follow this command format:

>Import-Module <module-name>

To illustrate, this command can be used to for a current session import of the module BitsTransfer:

>Import-Module BitsTransfer

A current session addition of the module TestCmdlets in the path C:\ps-test can be done with the following command:

>Import-Module C:\ps-test\TestCmdlets

To be more specific, a current session addition of the module TestCmdlets.dll in the path C:\ps test can be done with this command:

>Import-Module C:\ps-test\TestCmdlets.dll

Import Module into Every Session

Module imports using the command Import-Module are only current session imports. Module imports for every starting PowerShell session require the addition of the command Import-Module into your profile.

Module Removal

Module removals result in the session deletion of commands added by the module. This command results in the session removal of a module:

>Remove-Module <module-name>

To illustrate, this command results in the session removal of the module BitsTransfer:

>Remove-Module BitsTransfer

Module removal reverses the module importing action. Module removal will not result in module uninstallation.

Name Conflicts and Modules

When multiple sessions share the same name, name conflicts occur. Module imports result in conflicts in names if commands from imported modules consist of names that are identical to items or commands within the session. Conflicts in name may have the impact of replacing and hiding commands.

Hidden

A hidden command does not run when only its name is typed as in a typical function or cmdlet call, but does run when another method is used, specifically when the command name is given additional qualifications from the source snap-in or module.

To illustrate, if a function identical to a cmdlet is imported into or defined in the session, then the cmdlet will be hidden because a module or snap-in was used to import it. This also follows from the command precedence rules of PowerShell.

The cmdlet will not be replaced; it may be still invoked using another method. For example, create a Get-Date function that invokes the Get-Date cmdlet, qualified with its source module without parameters, as follows:

```
function Get-Date {

$date = Microsoft.PowerShell.Utility\Get-Date

$date

}
```

The Get-Date cmdlet is now hidden by the function of the same name. Invoking the Get-Command cmdlet with the Get-Date command as the Name parameter produces the following output:

```
> Get-Command Get-Date
```

CommandType	Name	ModuleName
Function	Get-Date	

The Get-Date cmdlet is only hidden because the invocation of the Get-Command cmdlet with the All parameter, which will display every available Get-Date command, generates the following output:

CommandType	Name	ModuleName
Function	Get-Date	
Cmdlet	Get-Date	Microsoft.PowerShell.Utility

Qualifying the cmdlet with the name of its source module Microsoft.PowerShell.Utility will invoke the cmdlet, not the function, as shown in the following command:

>Microsoft.PowerShell.Utility\Get-Date

05 February 2020 10:40:41 PM

Replaced

A replaced command cannot be run since an identically-named command has overwritten it. Even after the removal of the conflict-causing module, the command replaced cannot be run unless the session is restarted. Import-Module can result in the replacement and addition of current session commands. Alternatively, session commands may cause the hiding of module introduced commands. Name conflicts may be detected through the use of parameter All of cmdlet Get-Command. The parameter All obtains all session commands that have a specific name.

Name conflicts can be prevented by using the Prefix parameter or calling NoClobber from the cmdlet Import-Module. The parameter Prefix appends name prefixes to commands that are imported so they become distinct within the session. The parameter NoClobber prevents commands from being imported that may result in the replacement or hiding of existing session commands.

The parameters Variable, Function, Cmdlet, and Alias of the cmdlet Import-Module can only be used in the selection of specific commands to be imported if these commands do not consist of name conflict-causing commands in the session.

To illustrate, if a function called Get-Map is imported into the session after a function Get-Map has been defined in the session, then the imported function replaces the original and the original function is no longer retrievable.

Snap-ins and Modules

Session commands may be added using snap-ins and modules. Modules are able to result in the addition of many command types, including variables, aliases, drives, functions, providers, and cmdlets.

Snap-ins are able to result only in the addition of providers and cmdlets.

Before making a session snap-in or module removal, these commands can be used for determining the commands to be taken away. This command determines the session cmdlet source:

>Get-Command <cmdlet-name> | Format-List -Property verb,noun,pssnapin,module

This command determines the cmdlet Get-Date source:

>Get-Command Get-Date | Format-List -Property verb,noun,module

Built-in Snap-ins and Modules

These snap-ins or modules are also installed alongside PowerShell installation:

- CimCmdlets
- Microsoft.PowerShell.Archive
- Microsoft.PowerShell.Core
- Microsoft.PowerShell.Diagnostics
- Microsoft.PowerShell.Host
- Microsoft.PowerShell.Management
- Microsoft.PowerShell.Security
- Microsoft.PowerShell.Utility

- Microsoft.WSMan.Management

- PackageManagement

- PowerShellGet

- PSDesiredStateConfiguration

- PSDiagnostics

- PSReadline

Providers

A provider is a program written within the .NET Framework specifically designed for making data within particular types of data stores accessible within PowerShell for managing and viewing it. Data made accessible by a provider displays as a file system drive and can be navigated on within using paths similar to navigating paths within disk drive. Built-in cmdlets supported by the provider can be used to help in managing data within a provider drive. Additionally, custom cmdlets specifically designed for data may be used.

Providers may supplement and enhance the functioning of built-in cmdlets dynamic parameters. Dynamic parameters are available only when cmdlets are used in managing the provider data classes.

Built-in providers

PowerShell has within it built-in providers that are utilized in the accessing of various classes of data. These are shown in Table 4 below.

Provider	Drive	Data store
Alias	Alias:	PowerShell aliases
Certificate	Cert:	x509 certificates for digital signatures
Environment	Env:	Windows environment variables
FileSystem	(*)	File system drives, directories, and files
Function	Function:	PowerShell functions
Registry	HKLM:, HKCU:	Windows registry
Variable	Variable:	PowerShell variables
WSMan	WSMan:	WS-Management configuration information

(*) **The FileSystem drives vary on each system.**

Table 4: PowerShell built-in providers

It is also possible for users to create custom PowerShell providers and install providers built by others. To display providers available in a session, use this command:

>Get-PSProvider

Provider Installation and Removal

Providers are normally installed within a current session by loading modules. Session providers are loaded by importing modules that also load the appropriate driver. Built-in providers cannot be uninstalled. It is, however, possible for providers to be uninstalled if they were loaded using the different modules.

A provider in the current session may be unloaded. This primarily performed using Remove-Module cmdlet. The provider will not be uninstalled from the environment by the Remove-Module cmdlet but will be made unavailable within the current session.

Alternatively, a drive in the current session may be removed. This primarily performed using Remove-PSDrive cmdlet. The data within the removed drive remains unchanged, but the drive will be unavailable in the session.

Viewing Providers

To display providers available on the local computer, enter the following command:

>Get-PSProvider

The output displays both built-in providers as well as any providers that were added during the session.

Provider cmdlets

After learning the proficiencies associated with the management of the specific data made accessible by one provider, the same techniques may be used to manage the class of data displayed by any provider. To illustrate, a new PowerShell item is created using the New-Item cmdlet. Similarly, the file system provider supports the C: drive, within which the New-Item cmdlet can be used to create a new file folder or file. The registry provider supports drives within which the New-Item cmdlet can be used to create registry keys. The alias prover supports the Alias:

drive, within which the New-Item cmdlet can be used to create a new alias.

This command can be used to display information this class of cmdlets:

>Get-Help <cmdlet-name> -Detailed

ChildItem cmdlets	Location cmdlets	ItemProperty cmdlets
Get-ChildItem	Get-Location	Clear-ItemProperty
	Pop-Location	Copy-ItemProperty
Content Cmdlets	Push-Location	Get-ItemProperty
Add-Content	Set-Location	Move-ItemProperty
Clear-Content		New-ItemProperty
Get-Content	**Path cmdlets**	Remove-ItemProperty
Set-Content	Join-Path	Rename-ItemProperty
	Convert-Path	Set-ItemProperty
Item Cmdlets	Split-Path	
Clear-Item	Resolve-Path	**PSProvider Cmdlets**
Copy-Item	Test-Path	Get-PSProvider
Get-Item		
Invoke-Item	**PSDrive cmdlets**	
Move-Item	Get-PSDrive	
New-Item	New-PSDrive	
	Remove-PSDrive	
Remove-Item		
Rename-Item		
Set-Item		

Table 5: PowerShell provider cmdlets

Viewing Provider Data

The primary benefit of a provider is its ability to expose data in a familiar and consistent way. The presentation model for the data is a file system drive. The data that the provider exposes is viewed, navigated through and changed as though it were data on a hard drive. The name of the drive that the provider supports is the most important information about the provider.

The default display of the Get-PSProvider cmdlet lists the drive, but information about the provider driver can be obtained using the Get-PSDrive cmdlet. To illustrate, the properties of the Function: drive can be obtained as follows:

>Get-PSDrive Function | Format-List *

The data displayed by a provider can be navigated analogously to how file system data is navigated on a drive, and managed. The contents in a drive exposed by a provider can be viewed using the Get-ChildItem or Get-Item cmdlets. The customary format for referring to a drive is the colon symbol (:) attached to the name of the drive. To illustrate, the Alias: drive holdings can be displayed with this command:

>Get-Item alias:

To manage and navigate drive data from another data drive, the managing provider cmdlet path parameter should include the name of the drive. To illustrate, the cmdlet Get-ChildItem command to view from within any drive the registry key HKLM\Software is as follows:

>Get-ChildItem HKLM:\SOFTWARE\

The cmdlet Set-location can be used to access a drive. The colon symbol (:) must be used in the drive path of this specification. To illustrate, to make the

Cert: drive root folder your current location from another location use this command:

>Set-Location cert:

Next, to display specific Cert: drive contents using the cmdlet Get-ChildItem, use this command:

>Get-ChildItem

Navigating Hierarchical Data Structures

The depicting architecture for navigating a drive displayed by a provider is the file system. Hierarchical drive contents can be navigated through the use of the backslash symbol \ to indicate that the following is a child item. The syntax is shown below:

>drive:\location\child-location\...

To illustrate, to make the key HKLM\software registry your present location, invoke a command using the cmdlet Set-Location, like:

>Set-Location HKLM:\SOFTWARE\

Double quotation marks should enclose all elements with a qualified full path name, including any spaces. To illustrate, an element with a qualified full path name with spaces is as follows:

>"C:\Program Files\Internet Explorer\iexplore.exe"

References that are relative for locations may also be used. A location that is current has a relative reference depicted by a dot symbol. To illustrate, if your target listing is registry subkeys within HKLM:\Software\Microsoft\PowerShell and your current location is the registry key HKLM\Software\Microsoft, use the following command:

> Get-ChildItem .\PowerShell

The relative reference from a location that is current to a container or directory directly above uses the double dot symbol (..). The paths, along with double dot symbol (..) and dot symbol (.), can be merged while navigating the hierarchy of the provider.

>PS C:\Windows\System32> cd "..\..\Program Files"

>PS C:\Program Files>

Provider Home

Providers similarly have a location that is Home. All PSDrives backed by the provider share this location. The provider property Home can be displayed to retrieve it. The Home default value property is unique to the provider of the FileSystem. This value is identical to $Home. The current session setting of a provider directory for Home can be performed using this command:

>Get-PSProvider | Format-Table Name, Home

Or:

>(Get-PSProvider FileSystem).Home = "C:\"

The home directory of a provider can be indicated using the symbol (~). If the provider location for Home is not set, the following error will be produced:

Cert:\> Set-Location ~

Set-Location : Home location for this provider is not set. To set the home

location, call "(get-psprovider 'Certificate').Home = 'path'".

At line:1 char:1

+ Set-Location ~

+ ~~~~~~~~~~~~~~~~

   + CategoryInfo   : InvalidOperation: (:) [Set-Location],

     PSInvalidOperationException

...

Dynamic Parameters

A dynamic parameter is a provider-added cmdlet parameter. The adding provider must be used jointly with the cmdlet for both to be available. To illustrate, the parameter CodeSigningCert is added to the Get-ChildItem and Get-Item cmdlets by the drive Cert:. This parameter can be only used with Get-ChildItem or Get-Item within the Cert drive.

Provider-supported dynamic parameters can be listed by displaying the provider Help file. The command is:

>Get-Help <provider-name>

To illustrate:

>Get-Help certificate

Help for Providers

Data provider drives can be navigated and displayed using similar methods to what we have been discussing, but in other aspects, they differ. The provider-exposed stores of data can vary from mailboxes to locations within the Active Directory. This command displays the help file for PowerShell providers:

>Get-Help <ProviderName>

To illustrate, for the registry provider:

>Get-Help registry

This command displays a listing of topics on provider Help topics:

>Get-Help * -Category Provider

Exercises

6.1. Why are modules important for administrators who write PowerShell commands?

6.2. How are PowerShell cmdlets and providers related to modules?

6.3. What cmdlet command is used to find modules installed in a default location but not yet imported into the PowerShell session?

6.4. What command is used to find modules that have been imported into the PowerShell session?

6.5. How are modules imported into every PowerShell session?

6.6. What is the command used to view default module locations?

6.7. What is a command name conflict and how is it caused by importing modules into the PowerShell session?

6.8. What do command name conflicts do in your PowerShell session?

6.9. List the PowerShell built-in providers.

6.10. What is the command used to view the providers in your computer?

6.11. What is the way to view and navigate through data in a provider?

6.12. What command is used to list the dynamic parameters that a provider supports?

Chapter Summary

The main points of the chapter were:

- A module is a grouping of PowerShell commands, such as cmdlets, providers, functions, workflows,variables and aliases.

- Modules are used by installing them and using the commands that the module added.

- Commands in a module can be used through module auto-loading.

- Modules are usually managed using cmdlets.

- Providers are .NET Framework-based programs for accessing data in specialized data stores.

- Providers are installed through modules.

- Providers are usually managed using cmdlets.

- Providers standardize the way in which data is accessed in PowerShell.

In the next chapter you will learn about scripting.

Chapter Seven:
Scripting

Scripting

In PowerShell, a plain text file with at least one command is called a script. Scripts in PowerShell have a .ps1 extension to their file name. Script execution is similar to cmdlet invocation. The path with the file name is typed, and parameters are used to set options and submit data values. Scripts can be run on either remote sessions or local ones. Script writing is useful because it stores a command for easy sharing and repeated use. An additional advantage is that command execution becomes a matter of file name submission with an accompanying script location path on the console. Scripts may be large intricate code structures or a simple one command directive.

There are supplementary features associated with a script, such as data support sections, parameter usage, security digital signing, and the special comment #Requires. Help topics can also be written for included functions as well as the script itself.

Running a Script

In PowerShell, script execution depends on execution policy. The PowerShell default policy for execution is "Restricted". This precludes all script execution, incorporating local computer authored scripts. This execution policy requires modification before script execution. The registry stores this policy, and its computer-based adjustment is one-time. This method can be used for modifying the PowerShell execution policy. Enter this command on the console:

>Set-ExecutionPolicy AllSigned

Alternatively:

>Set-ExecutionPolicy RemoteSigned

The modification takes effect instantaneously. Submit the complete path as well as then name for script execution. To illustrate, to execute the script Get-ServiceLog.ps1 with path C:\Script, the command is:

>C:\Scripts\Get-ServiceLog.ps1

A current directory script execution requires either a dot symbol (.) current directory representation or a current directory complete path followed by a backslash symbol \ for path. To illustrate, the command to execute a current location script called ServiceLog.ps1 is:

>.\Get-ServiceLog.ps1

If parameters are part of the script, submit the parameter values and their names following the file name of the script. To illustrate, this command makes use of the parameter ServiceName within the script Get-ServiceLog for a service activity log request belonging to WinRM:

>.\Get-ServiceLog.ps1 -ServiceName WinRM

A PowerShell security feature is that scripts will not run when you double-click the script icon in the file explorer or when you type the script name without the full path, even if the script is in the current directory.

Run With Option

Introduced in Windows PowerShell 3.0, the File Explorer can be used to run scripts by using the "run with PowerShell" feature.

The feature may be used as follows:

Open File Explorer, right-click on script and select the PowerShell option.

This feature is intended for script execution that does not generate console output and for scripts without required parameters.

Remote Execution

Remote script execution can be conducted using the parameter FilePath of the cmdlet Invoke-Command. The complete file name and path can be submitted as a FilePath parameter value. The script has to be housed on a local path or a locally accessible folder. This command executes the script Get-ServiceLog.ps1 two remote computers(ServerA and ServerB):

>Invoke-Command   -ComputerName
ServerA,ServerB -FilePath `

　　C:\Scripts\Get-ServiceLog.ps1

Script Help

The cmdlet Get-Help obtains help topics for cmdlets, other command types and scripts.

A script help topic may be displayed by invoking the Get-Help cmdlet with the script name and script path as the Name parameter value. The path may be omitted if the path of the script is part of the environment variable PATH.

To illustrate, the script ServiceLog.ps1 help file may be displayed with this command:

>get-help C:\admin\scripts\ServicesLog.ps1

Writing a Script

All valid PowerShell commands may be housed in a script consisting of functions, control structures, pipeline commands, and single commands.

A script may be written as follows:

1. Open a script editor (VS Code) or text editor (Notepad).

2. Enter script commands.

3. Save commands within a file with .ps1 name extension and valid name.

The following illustration is a script that obtains running local system services and writes them into file. A current date variable is used to create the file name:

```
$date = (get-date).dayofyear

get-service | out-file "$date.log"
```

The script can be created using a script or text editor.

Script Parameters

A script parameter functions similarly to a function parameter. All script commands can access the values of the parameters. Every function parameter feature has validity in scripts. When the script is executed, parameters are supplied following the name of the script.

This example illustrates a script named Test-Remote.ps1 with a ComputerName parameter. The value of the ComputerName parameter is accessible to both functions of the script. This script can be executed by entering the name of the parameter following the name of the script. To illustrate:

```
Test-Remote.ps1

param ($ComputerName = $(throw
"ComputerName parameter is required."))

function CanPing {
```

174

```
$error.clear()

$tmp = test-connection $computername -
erroraction SilentlyContinue

if (!$?)

{write-host "Ping attempt failed:
$ComputerName."; return $false}

else

{write-host "Ping attempt succeeded:
$ComputerName"; return $true}

}

function CanRemote {

$s = new-pssession $computername -
erroraction SilentlyContinue

if ($s -is
[System.Management.Automation.Runspaces.PSSessi
on])

{write-host "Remote test succeeded:
$ComputerName."}

else

{write-host "Remote test failed:
$ComputerName."}

}

if (CanPing $computername) {CanRemote
$computername}
```

This script can be run by typing the parameter name after the script name. To illustrate, enter the following in PowerShell:

> .\test-remote.ps1 -computername localhost

Ping attempt succeeded: localhost

Remote test failed: localhost

Help for Scripts

Use the .ExternalHelp Help comment keyword to associate the script with the XML-based help topic. A script help topic may be written by making use of either of the following two methods:

- Script Comment-Based Help: Comment-special keywords may be used to create topics for the help file. Script comment-based Help may be created by placing comments at the end or beginning of the file of the script.

- Script XML-Based Help: A topic XML-based Help may be created, such as the type usually generated for cmdlets. This is a requirement when translating topics for help into different languages.

The topic XML-based Help may be related to the script using the comment .ExternalHelp Help keyword.

Dot Sourcing and Script Scope

Each script executes within its individual scope. The scope of the script is the only place where the variables, functions, drives, and aliases specified within the script are defined. The values of these items and the items themselves cannot be accessed outside the script scope.

A script may be run in another scope by specifying a scope, such as Local or Global, or by dot sourcing the script. Dot sourcing allows a script to be executed within the local scope rather than within its scope. When a dot sourced script is executed, the script commands run as if they were entered on the console. The aliases, variables, drives, and functions created by the script are defined within the local scope. After running the script in the session, the values of the items created by the script may be accessed and the items created by the script may be used.

A script may be dot sourced by typing a dot symbol (.) followed by a space and then the path to the script. To illustrate:

>. C:\Scripts\TestValue.ps1

Or, if your location is the C:\Scripts folder:

>. .\TestValue.ps1

177

While the script executes, the variable $ProfileName and function New-Profile exist. The variable and function will be deleted after the script stops executing, as illustrated in the following example:

#In TestValueFunction.ps1

function New-TestValue

{

param ([int]$one)

Write-Host "Running New-TestValue function"

$TestVariable = $one

$TestVariable

}

$TestVariable_1 =20

When the script is executed using dot sourcing, the variables $TestVariable_1 and $ProfileName and the function New-Profile are created by the script within the local scope. The function New-TestValue can be used within the session, as illustrated with this example.

> C:\Scripts\TestValue.ps1

> New-TestValue 10

New-TestValue : The term 'New-TestValue' is not recognized as the name of a cmdlet, function, script file, or operable program. Check the spelling of the name, or if a path was included, verify that the path is correct and try again.

At line:1 char:1

+ New-TestValue 10

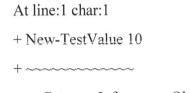

+ ~~~~~~~~~~~~~~~~

+ CategoryInfo   : ObjectNotFound: (New-TestValue:String) [], CommandNotFoundException

+   FullyQualifiedErrorId   : CommandNotFoundException

PS C:\>

After the script has run, you can use the New-TestValue function and access the TestVariable_1 variable in your session, as shown in the following example:

>C:\Scripts\TestValue.ps1

>New-TestValue 10

Running New-TestValue function

10

>TestVariable_1

20

Scripts in Modules

A collection of associated PowerShell resources which may be delivered as a group is a module. Modules may be used to arrange functions, other resources, and scripts. Modules may be used to deliver programs and access programs from trusted sources. Scripts may be included in modules, or alternatively, a new module called the script module may be created. A script module is made up primarily or entirely of a script file and its supporting resources. A script file with a name extension .psm1 is a script module.

Other Features of Scripts

PowerShell offers a variety of beneficial features that may be used within scripts:

- #Requires: It is possible to make use of a statement called #Requires, which precludes a script executing without a stipulated PowerShell version and snap-ins or modules.

- $PSCommandPath: This has the complete name and path of the executing script. This is a valid parameter in every script. This variable, which is automatic, was established as part of Windows PowerShell 3.0.

- $PSScriptRoot: This has the folder from within a script that is executing. This variable was established as part of Windows PowerShell 3.0.

- $MyInvocation: This variable, which is automatic, has information on the executing script, as well as information concerning the manner in which it was invoked or started. This variable, as well as its characteristics, may be used to obtain information concerning the script while the script executes. $MyInvocation.MyCommand.Path has the file name and path belonging to the script. $MyInvocation.Line has the command which begins the execution of the script, as well as every value and parameter associated with it.

  Starting with Windows PowerShell 3.0, the $MyInvocation variable contains two additional properties that hold information on the script that invoked or called the executing script. These property values become filled in the circumstance that a script is the caller or invoker.

- PSCommandPath: This has the complete name and full path belonging to the script which invoked or called the executing script.

- PSScriptRoot: This has the folder belonging to the script which invoked or called the executing script.

- Data sections: The keyword Data may be used to demarcate logic from data within scripts.

Data sections are also able to make localization less difficult.

- Script Signing: A digital signature may be added to a file that is a script. Contingent on the specific execution policy it is possible to make use of digital signatures in precluding the execution of scripts which may have within them commands that are not safe.

Note: It is crucial that you do not confuse the following. $PSScriptRoot and $PSCommandPath are automatic variables. They hold information on the executing script. PSScriptRoot and PSCommandPath are properties belonging to the variable $MyInvocation. They hold information on the script that called the currently executing one.

Script Blocks

A set of expressions or statements that can be operated as one item is called script block. A script block is able to return values and accept arguments. Functionally, the script block constitutes a list of statements enclosed in brace symbols {} and has the following syntax:

{<statement list>}

A script block returns the output of all commands in the script block either as a single object or as an array of objects. A return value can be specified using the return keyword. The return keyword does not affect or suppress other output returned from the script block, but it does exit the script block at that line.

The script block, in a similar manner to functions, may include parameters. The Param keyword is used for assigned parameters that are named, as is shown in this syntax:

```
{
Param([type]$Parameter1 [,[type]$Parameter2])
<statement list>
}
```

It is important to note that, in contrast to a function, it is not possible for the script block to define parameters externally of the braces. Similar to functions, the keywords DynamicParam, Process, Begin and End may be included in script blocks.

Script Block Use

A script block is an instance of a Microsoft .NET Framework type System.Management.Automatioc.ScriptBlock class. Commands can also have script block parameter values. To illustrate, the Invoke-Command cmdlet has a ScriptBlock parameter that takes a script block value, as shown in the following command:

```
>Invoke-Command -ScriptBlock { Get-Process }
```

The next call will generate the following output (of which only the first few lines are shown):

PS C:\> Invoke-Command -ScriptBlock { Get-Process }

Handles	NPM(K)	PM(K)	WS(K)	CPU(s)	Id	SI	ProcessName
504	30	22352	23204	1.42	43796	0	AbtSvcHost_
370	18	3880	2300	3.23	3532	0	armsvc
133	9	2380	952	0.11	15092	0	CNTAoSMgr
116	7	5332	860	0.02	2084	0	conhost
146	10	7588	1180	8,278.19	4928	0	conhost
146	10	7600	2116	9,121.56	4948	0	conhost
146	10	7632	1072	8,554.69	5404	0	conhost
116	7	5316	696	0.11	35556	0	conhost
239	13	4592	1395	18.05	5104	21	conhost

		2			8	6	
137	9	5596	5444	0.61	5521 6	0	conhost
905	26	2012	1924	216.64	724	0	csrss

The Invoke-Command cmdlet is also able to run script blocks, which hold parameter blocks. The parameter ArgumentList can be used to assign parameters by position:

>Invoke-Command -ScriptBlock { param($p1, $p2)

"p1: $p1"

"p2: $p2"

} -ArgumentList "First", "Second"

Which will generate the following output:

PS C:\> Invoke-Command -ScriptBlock { param($p1, $p2)

>> "p1: $p1"

>> "p2: $p2"

>> } -ArgumentList "First", "Second"

p1: First

p2: Second

PS C:\>

Variables can be used to store and execute script blocks. In the following command sequence, the first command stores a script block in a variable $a, and the second command passes $a to the Invoke-Command cmdlet:

>$a = { Get-Service BITS }

>Invoke-Command -ScriptBlock $a

This will generate the following output:

PS C:\> $a = { Get-Service BITS }

PS C:\> Invoke-Command -ScriptBlock $a

Status   Name   DisplayName

------   ----   -----------

Running BITS   Background Intelligent Transfer Ser...

This script block considered in the example just considered makes use of the keyword param to define two parameters. The $p1 parameter is made to be bound to the "First" string and the parameter $p2 is analogously made to be bound to the "Second" string. Variables may be used to execute and store script blocks. The example below shows how this may be done:

>$a ={ param($p1, $p2)

"p1: $p1"

"p2: $p2"

186

}

>&$a -p2 "First" -p1 "Second"

This will generate the following output:

PS C:\> $a ={ param($p1, $p2)

>> "p1: $p1"

>> "p2: $p2"

>> }

PS C:\> &$a -p2 "First" -p1 "Second"

p1: Second

p2: First

PS C:\>

Another method to run script blocks that are housed within a variable is by making use of the call operator. Similar to the Invoke-Command cmdlet, it runs a script block within a nested child scope. It may facilitate a less difficult method for the use of parameters within script blocks.

Example: Saving output from script block execution with call operator

The following sequence of commands:

>$a = { 1 + 1}

>$b = &$a

>$b

It will generate the following output:

2

Example: Saving output from script block execution with the Invoke-Command cmdlet

The following sequence of commands:

>$a = { 1 + 1}

>$b = Invoke-Command $a

>$b

It will generate the following output:

2

It is possible to store the returns from the script block within a variable by making use of assignments.

Delay-bind type script blocks

Delay-bind type script blocks are used on parameters that are typed which accept pipeline input by PropertyName or Value. The object that is piped in can be referenced within the delay-bind type script block with the use of the pipeline type variable $.

This is illustrated by the following pipeline command, which appends old_ to the name of the files in directory config.log:

># Renames config.log to old_config.log

>dir config.log | Rename-Item -NewName {"old_" + $_.Name}

It is important to note the following concerning delay-bind type script blocks being parameters:

- All parameters names used within delay-bind type script blocks must be plainly specified.

- The parameter may not be type [object] or [scriptblock] and cannot be untyped.

- An error will be received if a delay-bind type script block is used when input from a pipeline is not provided.

This concept is illustrated in this example and its resulting output:

```
>Rename-Item -NewName {$_.Name + ".old"}
```

will lead to the error shown below:

```
PS C:\> Rename-Item -NewName {$_.Name + ".old"}
```

Rename-Item : Cannot evaluate parameter 'NewName' because its argument is specified as a script block and there is no input. A script block cannot be evaluated without input.

At line:1 char:22

+ Rename-Item -NewName {$_.Name + ".old"}

+   ~~~~~~~~~~~~~~~~~~~

    + CategoryInfo   : MetadataError: (:) [Rename-Item], ParameterBindingException

+ FullyQualifiedErrorId :
ScriptBlockArgumentNoInput,Microsoft.PowerShell.
Commands.RenameItemCommand

Exercises

7.1. What is the file name extension for PowerShell scripts?

7.2. Why are scripts useful when running commands?

7.3. Why is it not possible to run a script on PowerShell's default execution policy?

7.4. What two commands can be used to change PowerShell's execution policy to one that can be used to run scripts on a local computer?

7.5. What command should you issue to get the help topics for a script?

7.6. How do you write a script?

7.7. How are parameters defined in a script?

7.8. How do you run a script in the current scope instead of the script scope?

7.9. What is a script module and what is its file name extension?

7.10. What is a script block?

Chapter Summary

The key points of the chapter were:

- A script is simply a plain text file containing one or more PowerShell commands.

- Scripts are basically run in PowerShell under the appropriate execution policy by typing the path and name of the script file.

- PowerShell scripts are written using a text editor or a script editor.

- Scripts can be enhanced through the creation comment-based or XML-based help for the script.

- Scripts run in script scope.

- A set of PowerShell statements or expressions can be used as a single unit using a script block.

In the next chapter you will learn about Remoting and the PowerShell Gallery.

Chapter Eight:
Remoting and PowerShell Gallery

This chapter considers Remoting and the PowerShell Gallery. Remoting involves the running of PowerShell commands and scripts on remote computers. The PowerShell Gallery is a central repository of PowerShell content and component of PowerShell.

In the first part of this chapter, we will look at Remoting; in the second part, we will consider the PowerShell Gallery.

Remoting

Remote commands may be run on many computers or a single computer through the use of either persistent or temporary connections. Two key parameters in PowerShell remoting are ComputerName and Session. The ComputerName parameter is designed for situations where a single command or several unrelated commands are run on one or many computers. The Session parameter establishes a persistent connection to a remote computer. This chapter will consider a set of illustrations that will demonstrate the various methods used in executing remote commands.

After attempting these basic commands, help topics can divulge additional information about the cmdlets used when running the following commands.

The help topics also explain and supply details and descriptions on how to modify these commands based on user needs and details.

Interactive Sessions

The simplest approach to executing a remote command is by starting an interactive session with a remote computer. At the start of the session, the remote commands execute on the computer that is remote similar to how direct commands on that remote computer would execute. In such an interactive session, only a single computer may connect. Using the cmdlet Enter-PSSession will start the interactive session. For example, to start an interactive session with computer Server01, use the following command:

>Enter-PSSession Server01

The Server01 computer connection is indicated by a command prompt change:

Server01\PS

At this stage, Server01 commands may be typed. To close the interactive session, use:

>Exit-PSSession

ComputerName Parameter Cmdlets

Many cmdlets include a parameter called ComputerName, which helps obtain objects from remote computers. Since WS-Management-based remoting within PowerShell is not used by this type of cmdlet, its ComputerName parameter can be used within all computers with PowerShell running. The remoting requirements of the system as well as PowerShell remoting configuration are not required on the computers.

The cmdlets that use the parameter ComputerName are shown in Table 6 below.

Cmdlets with ComputerName parameter	
Clear-EventLog	Get-WmiObject
Get-Counter	Limit-EventLog
Get-EventLog	New-EventLog
Get-HotFix	Remove-EventLog
Get-Process	Restart-Computer
Get-Service	Show-EventLog
Get-WinEvent	Stop-Computer
Write-EventLog	Test-Connection

Table 6: Remoting cmdlets

To illustrate, the following command displays the services that are on the remote computer Server01:

>Get-Service -ComputerName Server01

In most cases, cmdlets supporting remoting exclusive of distinctive configurations include a ComputerName parameter but not a Session parameter. These may be displayed in the session with this command:

>Get-Command | Where-Object {

$_.Parameters.Keys -contains 'ComputerName' -and

$_.Parameters.Keys -notcontains 'Session'

}

This will generate the following output (of which the first few lines are shown):

```
PS C:\Test> Get-Command | Where-Object {

>>

>>        $_.Parameters.Keys        -contains
'ComputerName' -and

>>

>>        $_.Parameters.Keys        -notcontains
'Session'

>>

>> }
```

Command Type	Name	Version	Source
-----------	----	-------	------
Cmdlet	Add-Computer	3.1.0.0	Microsoft.PowerShell.Management

Cmdlet	Clear-EventLog	3.1.0.0	Microsoft.PowerShell.Management
Cmdlet	Get-EventLog	3.1.0.0	Microsoft.PowerShell.Management
Cmdlet	Get-HotFix	3.1.0.0	Microsoft.PowerShell.Management
Cmdlet	Get-Process	3.1.0.0	Microsoft.PowerShell.Management
Cmdlet	Get-PSSession	3.0.0.0	Microsoft.PowerShell.Core
Cmdlet	Get-Service	3.1.0.0	Microsoft.PowerShell.Management
Cmdlet	Get-WmiObject	3.1.0.0	Microsoft.PowerShell.Management
Cmdlet	Invoke-WmiMethod	3.1.0.0	Microsoft.PowerShell.Management

Running Remote Commands

The cmdlet Invoke-Command is used to execute other commands within remote computers. A limited number of unrelated commands or a single command may be run using the parameter ComputerName within the Invoke-Command cmdlet to denote the computers that are remote. The parameter ScriptBlock may be used to define the command.

To illustrate, this command executes a command designated Get-Culture within the computer Server01:

>Invoke-Command -ComputerName Server01 -ScriptBlock {Get-Culture}

Persistent Connection

When the cmdlet Invoke-Command ComputerName parameter is used, PowerShell will establish a connection only for the purposes of the command. The connection is closed as soon as the command has executed. All functions or variables the command defined are lost. The cmdlet New-PSSession can be used to create a connection that is persistent to a computer that is remote. To illustrate, this command is used to create PSSessions on computers ServerA and ServerB, and then store them in the variable $s:

>$s = New-PSSession -ComputerName ServerA, ServerB

Running Commands in PSSession

A PSSession is used to execute a remote collection of commands that share data. This data may take the shape of variable values, aliases, and functions. PSSession commands may be executed using the parameter Session of the cmdlet Invoke-Command. To illustrate, the following command uses the cmdlet Invoke-Command to execute the command Get-Process within the PSSessions established on computers ServerA and ServerB. The processes are saved in a variable $p by the command in each of the PSSessions.

>Invoke-Command -Session $s -ScriptBlock {$p = Get-Process}

Since a persistent connection is used by the PSSession, another command may be executed within the identical PSSession using the variable $p. This command generates a count of the processes saved in the variable $p.

>Invoke-Command -Session $s -ScriptBlock {$p.count}

Running Remote Commands on Many Computers

A command that is remote may be run on many computers by typing their computer names within the ComputerName parameter value of the Invoke-Command cmdlet using a comma to separate computer names. To illustrate, this command is used to run a command designated Get-Culture within three computers:

>Invoke-Command -ComputerName S1, S2, S3 -ScriptBlock {Get-Culture}

A command may also be run in many PSSessions. These commands create PSSessions on three computers and then executes a command designated Get-Culture within each PSSession:

>$s = New-PSSession -ComputerName S1, S2, S3

>Invoke-Command -Session $s -ScriptBlock {Get-Culture}

A local computer may be included in the computer list by typing its name, in which case the local computer's designation will be localhost or the dot symbol:

>Invoke-Command -ComputerName S1, S2, S3, localhost -ScriptBlock {Get-Culture}

Remotely Running a Script

A script that is local may be run on computers that are remote by using the InvokeCommand cmdlet FilePath parameter. To illustrate, this command executes the script Sample.ps1 on two computers:

>Invoke-Command -ComputerName Server01, Server02 -FilePath C:\Test\Sample.ps1

The script execution results are sent to the computer that is local. It is not necessary to copy files.

Stopping Remote Commands

A remote command may be interrupted by pressing CTRL+C. The request for an interruption is sent to the computer that is remote where it stops the command that is remote.

PowerShell Gallery

The PowerShell content central repository is known as PowerShell Gallery or simply Gallery. Within it, DSC resources and modules containing commands may be found. It is also possible to find scripts. The Gallery packages are authored within the PowerShell community and Microsoft.

PowerShellGet

The module PowerShellGet has cmdlets for publishing, installing, discovering, and updating PowerShell packages from the central repository and other private repositories. These packages house artifacts such as DSC resources, modules, scripts, and role capabilities.

Getting Started: PowerShell Gallery

Gallery package installations require an updated version of PowerShellGet, which is part of PowerShell7.0. MacOS, Linux, and Windows all support PowerShellGet operation.

Latest version of PowerShellGet

Install the updated version of the NuGet provider before looking to update PowerShellGet. This is done with the following commands:

>Install-PackageProvider -Name NuGet -Force

>Exit

Then, run these commands:

>Install-Module -Name PowerShellGet -Force

>Exit

The Update-Module cmdlet should be used to obtain updated versions. This can be done with this command:

>Update-Module -Name PowerShellGet

>Exit

PowerShell Gallery Overview

PowerShellGet cmdlets may be used for installing packages from within PowerShell Gallery. The Gallery may be used without first signing in to obtain PowerShell content. The Gallery may also be used to download packages directly; however, this method is not suggested.

Discovering Packages

Gallery packages can be found by making use of the search facility in the Gallery home page or by exploring scripts and modules in the packages page. Packages may also be found using the Find-Script, Find-DSCResource, and Find-Module cmdlets with the Repository parameter value PSGallery.

Gallery results may be filtered by using the following parameters:

- AllVersions
- Filter
- Name
- MinimumVersion
- RequiredVersion
- Tag
- Includes
- RoleCapability
- DscResource
- Command

The Find-DscResource cmdlet may be used for discovering particular DSC resources within the Gallery. The cmdlet displays information about DSC resources housed within the Gallery. DSC resources are delivered using modules. It is necessary to use the Install-Module cmdlet to install DSC resources.

Learning about PowerShell Gallery Packages

Once a package is identified, it may be necessary to learn about it more. This may be done by examining the package page within the Gallery. The page may be used to display metadata on the package. The metadata is supplied by the package author.

The other method is by using the Find-Script or Find-Module cmdlets to display the PSGetModuleInfo object. To illustrate, this command displays Gallery data about the module PSReadLine:

>Find-Module -Name PSReadLine -Repository | Get-Member

Downloading PowerShell Gallery packages

This is the suggested manner with which to download packages contained in the Gallery:

- Inspect:

  The Save-Script or Save-Module cmdlets may be used for downloading a Gallery package for examination. This method allows for the package to be saved locally without installation. Once saved locally, its contents may be reviewed.

- Install:

1. Install-Module

The default installation path for Install-Module is:

$env:ProgramFiles\WindowsPowerShell\Module
s.

Administrator access is required to install modules in this path. If the Scope parameter in the Install-Module cmdlet is set to value CurrentUser, the module installation path will be:

$env:USERPROFILE\Documents\WindowsPowe rShell\Modules

2. Install-Scripts

The default installation path for Install-Script is:

$env:ProgramFiles\WindowsPowerShell\Scripts

Administrator access is needed to install scripts to this path.

If the Scope parameter in the Install-Script cmdlet is set

to value CurrentUser, the script installation path will be:

$env:USERPROFILE\Documents\WindowsPowe rShell\Scripts

Install-Script and Install-Module, by default, install the latest version of a specified package.The RequiredVersion parameter value can be used to install a specific version.

Package Update

Packages installed from the gallery may be updated by running either the [Update-Script][] or [Update-Module][] cmdlets. When the [Update-Script][] cmdlet is invoked without parameters, it will try updating all scripts that were installed by invoking the Install-Script cmdlet. The Name parameter may be used to update specific scripts. Analogously for modules, [Update-Module][] will try updating all modules that were installed using the Install-module cmdlet. The Name parameter may also be used to update specific modules.

List Packages installed from PowerShell Gallery

The Get-InstalledModule cmdlet may be used to determine the modules that were installed from the Gallery. This command displays all modules in the system obtained directly from the Gallery. Analogously for scripts, the Get-InstalledScripts cmdlet may be used to ascertain the scripts that were installed from the Gallery. This command, analogously to modules, will display all scripts in the system obtained directly from the Gallery.

Exercises

8.1. What cmdlet is used to start an interactive session on a computer?

8.2. How many cmdlets have a ComputerName parameter in PowerShell 7.0?

8.3. How is remote command run using the Invoke-Command cmdlet?

8.4. What cmdlet is used to create a persistent connection to a remote computer?

8.5. How are commands run in persistent connection?

8.6. How are local scripts run on remote computers?

8.7. What module is used to acquire PowerShell content from the PowerShell Gallery?

8.8. What type of content is contained in PowerShell Gallery packages?

8.9. What command is used to install the latest NuGet provider in PowerShell?

8.10. What command is used to install the latest version of PowerShellGet in PowerShell?

8.11. What cmdlet is used to update modules installed from the PowerShell Gallery?

8.12. What cmdlet is used to update scripts installed from the PowerShell Gallery?

8.13. What cmdlet is used to obtain a list of all modules installed from the PowerShell Gallery?

8.14. What cmdlet is used to obtain a list of all scripts installed from the PowerShell Gallery?

Chapter Summary

The key points of the chapter were:

- PowerShell commands can be run remotely on a single computer or collection of computers.

- The easiest way to run remote commands is through an interactive session.

- A more efficient way to run remote commands is through a persistent connection.

- Remoting allows for PowerShell scripts to be run remotely.

- PowerShell Gallery is a central repository for PowerShell content.

- The PowerShellGet module contains cmdlets that are used for discovering, installing, and publishing PowerShell packages.

Answers to Exercises

1.1. PowerShell can be run using command line options from another tool such as Cmd.exe or bash or by starting a new session on the PowerShell command line.

1.2. PowerShell, .NET Core and C#.

1.3. Yes, by using the PowerShell extension.

1.4. PowerShellGet module.

1.5 It is a package repository containing scripts, modules, and Desired State Configuration (DSC) resources can be downloaded and leveraged.

1.6. VS Code --install-extension command line switch providing the path a .vsix file. as follows: code --install-extension <File path>/myextension.vsix

2.1. 15

2.2. In simple terms, cmdlets perform an action and typically return a Microsoft .NET Framework object to the next command in the pipeline.

2.3. It makes it possible to perform customized administrative actions in PowerShell.

2.4. Implementing a cmdlet class that derives from one of two specialized cmdlet base classes.

2.5. Verb and Noun specification to invoke the cmdlet.

2.6. 35

2.7. Using command syntax diagrams.

2.8. Aliases are alternate names for cmdlets or command elements such as a function, script, file, or executable file.

2.9. 5. They are Get-Alias, New-Alias, Set-Alias, Export-Alias, and Import-Alias.

2.10. Get-Help cmdlet.

3.1. A unit of memory in which values are stored.

3.2. Text strings that start with a dollar ($) sign.

3.3. These may be difficult to use.

3.4. No.

3.5. Yes.

3.6. Using the Get-Variable cmdlet.

3.7. Variables are not limited to specific types of objects.

3.8. By the .NET types of the values of the variables.

3.9. Enclose the variable name with curly braces {}.

3.10. Variables are only available in the scope in which they are created.

3.11. Using the PowerShell Variable provider. It behaves similar to a file system drive. Contains PowerShell variables in your session and their values.

3.12. With command: Get-Command -Noun Variable

4.1. Using a pipeline operator.

4.2. Left to right.

4.3. As a single operation.

4.4. By-Value or By-PropertyName.

4.5.Parameters must be able to accept input from a pipeline. Parameters must be able to accept the type of object sent or a type that can be converted to the expected type. Parameters are not used in the command.

4.6. One at a time.

5.1. As if typed on the command prompt.

5.2. Yes, named, positional, switch and dynamic.

5.3. Command line or from the pipeline.

5.4. A Function keyword, a scope (optional), a name that you select, any number of named parameters (optional), and one or more PowerShell commands enclosed in braces {}

5.5. Any.

5.6. A function only exists in the scope in which it was created.

5.7. Automatically stores all functions and filters in PowerShell.

6.1. Modules allow administrators who write commands to organize them and share them with others.

6.2. All cmdlets and providers in a PowerShell session are added by a module or a snap-in.

6.3. Get-Module -ListAvailable

6.4. Get-Module

6.5. By adding the Import-Module command into your PowerShell profile.

6.6. $Env:PSModulePath

6.7. A name conflict is when more than one command has the same name. Name conflicts are caused by importing modules when the imported module has commands that have the same name as other commands or items in the session.

6.8. They can result in important commands being hidden or replaced.

6.9. Alias, Certificate, Environment, FileSystem, Function, Registry, Variable and WSMan.

6.10. Get-PSProvider

6.11. The same way you would data on a file system drive.

6.12. Get-Help <provider-name>

7.1. .ps1

7.2. Commands in a script can be run simply by typing the script path and file name.

7.3. The default PowerShell execution policy is "restricted," and prevents all scripts from running, including those written on the local computer.

7.4. Set-ExecutionPolicy AllSigned , Set-Executionpolicy RemoteSigned

7.5. get-help <path to script>\<ScriptName>.ps1

7.6. Using a text editor (such as Notepad) or a script editor (such as VS Code).

7.7. Using the Param keyword.

7.8. Using dot sourcing.

7.9. A script module is a module that consists entirely or primarily of a script and supporting resources. .psm1

7.10. A set of statements or expressions that can be used as a single unit.

8.1. Enter-PSSession cmdlet

8.2. 16

8.3. Using the ComputerName and ScriptBlock parameters.

8.4. New-PSSession cmdlet

8.5. Using the Invoke-Command cmdlet with the Session and ScriptBlock parameters.

8.6. Using the Invoke-Command cmdlet with the ComputerName and FilePath parameters.

8.7. PowerShellGet module.

8.8. Modules, DSC resources, role capabilities, and scripts.

8.9. Install-PackageProvider -Name NuGet -Force

8.10. Install-Module -Name PowerShellGet -Force

8.11. [Update-Module][] cmdlet

8.12. [Update-Script][] cmdlet

8.13. Get-InstalledModule cmdlet

8.14. Get-InstalledScript cmdlet

Final Words

In this book we covered beginner PowerShell concepts in a comprehensive manner. The tour included an introduction to the main components of PowerShell and the main tools available for using PowerShell to do computer systems administration. The tools considered included cmdlets, commands, variables, functions, pipelines, modules, providers, scripting, package management, and remoting. This introductory book also provided a means to access and develop other PowerShell tools. These means included an elementary introduction to the .NET Core SDK which can be used for developing custom cmdlets, modules and providers.

References

"2019 – Powershell". 2019. *Devblogs.Microsoft.Com.*
https://devblogs.microsoft.com/powershell/201
9/feed/.

"About_Aliases - Powershell". 2020.
Docs.Microsoft.Com.
https://docs.microsoft.com/en-
us/powershell/module/microsoft.powershell.co
re/about/about_aliases?view=powershell-7.

"About_Command_Syntax - Powershell". 2020.
Docs.Microsoft.Com.
https://docs.microsoft.com/en-
us/powershell/module/microsoft.powershell.co
re/about/about_command_syntax?view=power
shell-7.

"About_Core_Commands - Powershell". 2020.
Docs.Microsoft.Com.
https://docs.microsoft.com/en-
us/powershell/module/microsoft.powershell.co
re/about/about_core_commands?view=powers
hell-7.

"About_Do - Powershell". 2019.
Docs.Microsoft.Com.
https://docs.microsoft.com/en-
us/powershell/module/microsoft.powershell.co
re/about/about_do?view=powershell-7.

"About_Foreach - Powershell". 2019.
Docs.Microsoft.Com.
https://docs.microsoft.com/en-
us/powershell/module/microsoft.powershell.co
re/about/about_foreach?view=powershell-7.

"About_Functions - Powershell". 2019.
Docs.Microsoft.Com.
https://docs.microsoft.com/en-
us/powershell/module/microsoft.powershell.co
re/about/about_functions?view=powershell-
7https://docs.microsoft.com/en-
us/powershell/module/microsoft.powershell.co
re/about/about_functions?view=powershell-7.

"About_If - Powershell". 2019. Docs.Microsoft.Com.
https://docs.microsoft.com/en-
us/powershell/module/microsoft.powershell.co
re/about/about_if?view=powershell-7.

"About_Modules - Powershell". 2019.
Docs.Microsoft.Com.
https://docs.microsoft.com/en-
us/powershell/module/microsoft.powershell.co
re/about/about_modules?view=powershell-7.

"About_Pipelines - Powershell". 2019.
Docs.Microsoft.Com.
https://docs.microsoft.com/en-
us/powershell/module/microsoft.powershell.co
re/about/about_pipelines?view=powershell-
7#investigating-pipeline-errors.

"About_Providers - Powershell". 2019. Docs.Microsoft.Com. https://docs.microsoft.com/en-us/powershell/module/microsoft.powershell.core/about/about_providers?view=powershell-7.

"About_Remote - Powershell". 2019. Docs.Microsoft.Com. https://docs.microsoft.com/en-us/powershell/module/microsoft.powershell.core/about/about_remote?view=powershell-7.

"About_Scopes - Powershell". 2019. Docs.Microsoft.Com. https://docs.microsoft.com/en-us/powershell/module/microsoft.powershell.core/about/about_scopes?view=powershell-7.

"About_Script_Blocks - Powershell". 2019. Docs.Microsoft.Com. https://docs.microsoft.com/en-us/powershell/module/microsoft.powershell.core/about/about_script_blocks?view=powershell-7.

"About_Script_Internationalization - Powershell". 2019. Docs.Microsoft.Com. https://docs.microsoft.com/en-us/powershell/module/microsoft.powershell.core/about/about_script_internationalization?view=powershell-7.

"About_Scripts - Powershell". 2019. Docs.Microsoft.Com. https://docs.microsoft.com/en-us/powershell/module/microsoft.powershell.core/about/about_scripts?view=powershell-7.

"About_Splatting - Powershell". 2019. Docs.Microsoft.Com. https://docs.microsoft.com/en-us/powershell/module/microsoft.powershell.core/about/about_splatting?view=powershell-7.

"About_Variables - Powershell". 2019. Docs.Microsoft.Com. https://docs.microsoft.com/en-us/powershell/module/microsoft.powershell.core/about/about_variables?view=powershell-7#variables-and-scope.

"About_While - Powershell". 2019. Docs.Microsoft.Com. https://docs.microsoft.com/en-us/powershell/module/microsoft.powershell.core/about/about_while?view=powershell-7.

"Announcing The Powershell 7.0 Release Candidate | Powershell". 2019. *Powershell*. https://devblogs.microsoft.com/powershell/announcing-the-powershell-7-0-release-candidate/.

Arntzen, Mike. 2019. "3 Reasons Why You Should Learn How To Use Powershell". Amaxra.Com. Accessed December 20. https://www.amaxra.com/blog/3-reasons-why-you-should-learn-how-to-use-powershell.

"Cmdlet Overview - Powershell". 2019. Docs.Microsoft.Com. https://docs.microsoft.com/en-us/powershell/scripting/developer/cmdlet/cmdlet-overview?view=powershell-7.

"Command (Computing)". 2019. En.Wikipedia.Org. https://en.wikipedia.org/wiki/Command_(computing).

"Get Started With The Powershell Gallery - Powershell". 2019. Docs.Microsoft.Com. https://docs.microsoft.com/en-us/powershell/scripting/gallery/getting-started?view=powershell-7.

"How To Write A Simple Cmdlet - Powershell". 2019. Docs.Microsoft.Com. https://docs.microsoft.com/en-us/powershell/scripting/developer/cmdlet/how-to-write-a-simple-cmdlet?view=powershell-7.

"Install .NET Core SDK On Windows, Linux, And Macos - .NET Core". 2019. Docs.Microsoft.Com. https://docs.microsoft.com/en-us/dotnet/core/install/sdk?pivots=os-linux#all-net-core-downloads.

"Install .NET Core SDK On Windows, Linux, And Macos - .NET Core". 2019. Docs.Microsoft.Com. https://docs.microsoft.com/en-us/dotnet/core/install/sdk?pivots=os-linux#all-net-core-downloads.

"Installing Powershell Core On Linux - Powershell". 2019. Docs.Microsoft.Com. https://docs.microsoft.com/en-us/powershell/scripting/install/installing-powershell-core-on-linux?view=powershell-7.

"Installing Powershell Core On Windows - Powershell". 2019. *Docs.Microsoft.Com.* https://docs.microsoft.com/en-us/powershell/scripting/install/installing-powershell-core-on-windows?view=powershell-7.

"Introducing .NET Standard | .NET Blog". 2016. *.NET Blog.* https://devblogs.microsoft.com/dotnet/introducing-net-standard/.

"Managing Extensions In Visual Studio Code". 2019. *Code.Visualstudio.Com.* https://code.visualstudio.com/docs/editor/extension-gallery.

".NET Core And Visual Studio Code". 2019. Code.Visualstudio.Com. https://code.visualstudio.com/docs/languages/dotnet.

"Online IT Training Videos, IT Certification Training | CBT Nuggets". 2019. *CBT Nuggets*. https://www.cbtnuggets.com/blog/certifications/microsoft/5-microsoft-certs-that-absolutely-require-powershell.

"Powershell Editing With Visual Studio Code". 2019. Code.Visualstudio.Com. https://code.visualstudio.com/docs/languages/powershell.

"Powershell Scripting - Powershell". 2019. *Docs.Microsoft.Com*. https://docs.microsoft.com/en-us/powershell/scripting/overview?view=powershell-7.

"Powershell". 2020. *En.Wikipedia.Org*. https://en.wikipedia.org/wiki/PowerShell.

"Running Visual Studio Code On Linux". 2019. Code.Visualstudio.Com. https://code.visualstudio.com/docs/setup/linux.

"Running Visual Studio Code On Macos". 2019. Code.Visualstudio.Com. https://code.visualstudio.com/docs/setup/mac.

"Running Visual Studio Code On Windows". 2019. Code.Visualstudio.Com. https://code.visualstudio.com/docs/setup/windows.

"Scripting Languages". 2018. *En.Wikipedia.Org*. https://en.wikipedia.org/wiki/Category:Scripting_languages.

"System Administrator". 2019. En.Wikipedia.Org. https://en.wikipedia.org/wiki/System_administrator.

"The Powershell Gallery - Powershell". 2019. Docs.Microsoft.Com. https://docs.microsoft.com/en-us/powershell/scripting/gallery/overview?view=powershell-7.